# Understand Selling

# Understand Selling

Target customers,
close deals,
win new sales

**KEN LANGDON**

**LONDON, NEW YORK, MUNICH, MELBOURNE, DELHI**

| | |
|---|---|
| Project Editor | Tom Broder |
| Project Art Editor | Edward Kinsey |
| Senior Editor | Simon Tuite |
| Senior Art Editor | Sara Robin |
| Assistant Editors | Amber Tokeley |
| | Tarda Davisoh-Aitkins |
| Assistant Designer | Kathryn Wilding |
| DTP Designer | Traci Salter |
| Production Controller | Stuart Masheter |
| Picture Researcher | Sarah Hopper |
| Special Photography | Roger Dixon |
| Executive Managing Editor | Adèle Hayward |
| Managing Art Editor | Karla Jennings |
| Art Director | Peter Luff |
| Publisher | Corinne Roberts |

First American Edition, 2007
Published in the United States by
DK Publishing, 375 Hudson Street,
New York, NY 10014

07 08 09 10   10 9 8 7 6 5 4 3 2 1

Copyright © 2006 Dorling Kindersley Limited
Text copyright © 2006 Ken Langdon

All rights reserved under International and Pan-American Copyright Conventions. No part of this publication may be reproduced, stored in a retrieval system, or transmitted in any form or by any means, electronic, mechanical, photocopying, recording or otherwise, without the prior written permission of the copyright owner. Published in Great Britain by Dorling Kindersley Limited.

A Cataloging-in-Publication record for this book is available from the Library of Congress.

ISBN 978-0-75662-615-0

ED248

DK books are available at special discounts for bulk purchases for sales promotions, premiums, fund-raising, or educational use. For details, contact: DK Publishing Special Markets, 375 Hudson Street, New York, NY 10014 or SpecialSales@dk.com

Printed and bound in China by Leo Paper Group

# Contents

## 1 Prepare For Your Customers

**14** Understand the Sales Relationship

**16** Make a Good First Impression

**18** Communicate Persuasively

**22** Identify Customer Benefits

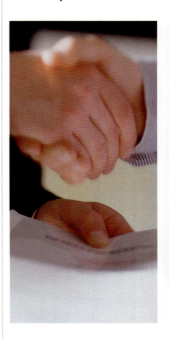

## 2 Find Your Customers

- **26** Know Your Market
- **30** Get Organized
- **32** The Sales Forecast
- **34** Find Your Prospects
- **42** Develop Your Sales Pipeline

## 3 Manage The Sales Process

- **46** Define the Sales Process
- **48** Plan the Initial Sales Call
- **50** Open the Sale
- **56** Qualify Your Prospects
- **60** Complete the Opening Call
- **64** Build the Sale
- **68** Make Your Proposal
- **70** Present Your Solution
- **74** Negotiate the Best Terms
- **78** Clinch the Deal
- **80** Protect Your Time

## 4 Deliver Customer Satisfaction

- **84** Put the Customer First
- **86** Satisfy Your Customers
- **90** Satisfy Your Retail Customers
- **94** Offer a First-Class Service

## 5 Manage Your Key Accounts

- **98** Focus on Your Best Customers
- **100** Build Your Account Team
- **102** The Key Account Process
- **104** Critical Success Factors
- **108** Write Your Key Account Plan
- **116** Complete Your Key Account Plan

- **118 Index**
- **120 Acknowledgments**

# Introduction

**No business can succeed without effective salespeople. Understanding professional salesmanship is, therefore, a key competency not only for front-line salespeople, but for anyone whose job in any way affects the most important asset any organization has—its customers.**

Professional sellers understand the necessity of making an excellent first impression. They know that a feature of their product only helps to make a sale if the customer can see how it will benefit them. And they understand each stage of the sales process, from the basics of questioning and listening to leading a customer toward saying "Yes, please—I'll buy it." So whether your customer is someone in a clothing store, a highly skilled buyer in a multinational, an entire board committee, or a middle manager controlling a budget, you need to develop the selling skills that will make more profitable sales quickly.

*Understand Selling* helps you to assess your current selling skills and then guides you through every aspect of the sales process, from effective opening techniques, through to the best ways to satisfy your customers and manage a sales team. It takes you from making the first telephone contact with a new prospect and planning your sales campaign to making the first sale and delivering your promises. It also looks at how to handle your key accounts—your most important customers, who typically supply up to 80 percent of an organization's total sales revenues—and tells you how to plan and manage such accounts to ensure customer loyalty and a growing stream of predictable, profitable sales.

> **Effective selling is the foundation of all business success**

Specially commissioned photographs illustrate the subtle visual signals a customer sends, and show you how to interpret and select the right technique for the right moment. There are also invaluable case studies, techniques that you can practice in your everyday life, professional tips, and special features on key aspects of the selling process—in short, everything you need to understand selling and become a top salesperson.

# Assessing Your Skills

The aim of this questionnaire is to get you to think about your selling skills and assess your scope for improvement, so answer honestly. Complete it before reading the book, choosing the answer that comes closest to your preferred response, and putting the appropriate letter in the "Before" box. After you have read the book and applied the techniques, complete the questionnaire a second time.

Before After

**1 How often do you use open questions?**
- **A** You are not sure what they are.
- **B** Whenever you meet a prospective customer.
- **C** Frequently throughout the selling cycle.

**2 How do you describe your products?**
- **A** In great detail, emphasizing the features that beat the competition.
- **B** You concentrate on the features that seem to interest the prospect.
- **C** You describe the features only in terms of their benefits to the prospect.

**3 How well do you establish the prospect's requirements?**
- **A** You assume all prospects need your products.
- **B** You ask them for their requirements early in the sales campaign.
- **C** You listen to their needs, summarize them back, and check regularly to see if they change.

**4 How accurate are your sales forecasts?**
- **A** It's impossible to forecast in your business.
- **B** You have months when they are quite accurate and others when they are miles out.
- **C** You usually hit your targets, within 10 percent.

| | Before | After |
|---|---|---|

### 5. How often do you set time aside for finding prospective customers?

- **A** You do it when you run out of them.
- **B** You do it from time to time.
- **C** You do it every week at different times.

### 6. What percentage of your time do you talk during an opening sales call?

- **A** Most of the time, to maximize selling time.
- **B** About fifty-fifty.
- **C** You aim for a balance of 20 percent you talking, with 80 percent from the prospect.

### 7. How well do you distinguish your offering from your competition's?

- **A** You can't in your business; the products are pretty much the same.
- **B** You know your products' USPs.
- **C** You can demonstrate USPs in your organization and your market position.

### 8. How well do you establish the prospect's basis of decision?

- **A** You are unfamiliar with the term.
- **B** You ask about the criteria at the first meeting.
- **C** You use the prospect's basis of decision as the framework of a sales campaign.

### 9. Do you maintain good records of contacts?

- **A** They're on a database.
- **B** You keep details until you have made a sale.
- **C** You keep your lifetime address book updated.

### 10. How do you complete an opening call?

- **A** You thank the prospect for his or her time and say that you will call back.
- **B** You explain the actions you are going to take following the meeting.
- **C** You agree on an action plan that always includes an action for the prospect to complete.

|  | Before | After |
|--|--|--|

### 11. Do you give discounts or other concessions?

- **A** Your starting price is the best you can make.
- **B** You start with the book terms and conditions, and offer what you can at the appropriate time.
- **C** You never give anything away unless it is vital to do so, and always show great reluctance.

### 12. How much time do you waste on prospects who do not, in the end, buy from you?

- **A** It happens all the time—that's selling.
- **B** If it becomes obvious that they are not going to buy, you drop the prospect.
- **C** You qualify prospects continuously and always explain your reasons to unqualified prospects.

### 13. How do you measure customer satisfaction?

- **A** You get a feel for it when complaints increase.
- **B** You get a few customers to fill in a customer satisfaction form at the end of each quarter.
- **C** You agree on customer satisfaction targets and use external and internal surveys.

### 14. How well do you know your key account's strategy, strengths, and weaknesses?

- **A** You don't need to in order to sell your products.
- **B** You ask the main buyer how business is going on a regular basis.
- **C** You have an agreed Account Development Plan that you keep up to date with this information.

## Final Scores

|  | A | B | C |
|--|--|--|--|
| **Before** |  |  |  |
| **After** |  |  |  |

# Analysis
## Mostly As
Your answers suggest that you are fairly new to selling and, while you may be enthusiastic, you need to think about the basic techniques of professional selling and the sales process. Consider first your contact with prospects and customers, and learn to listen more. Then work on the selling process to ensure that you understand each stage and are confident how far down the selling track you are at any point in time. Think more about your customers and what they need and want.

## Mostly Bs
You have some knowledge of professional selling and deal with your prospects and customers quite well. You are starting to see the sale from the customer's point of view, but you need to put more time and energy into improving your skills in this area. Start with one customer and one sales campaign and plan your way through each stage in the process. Be self-critical of your overall approach to a key account.

## Mostly Cs
You certainly have a professional approach to your role as a salesperson. Make sure, however, that you establish good rapport with customers as well as treating them professionally. Concentrate on the long-term strategy and use some of the techniques in this book to help build mutually profitable relationships. Use these techniques to assist other people in your team to improve their skills. Show them how important it is to have open and honest contacts with prospects and customers.

# Conclusion
If this is the first time you have done this self-assessment, then bear in mind the above analysis as you read the book. Pay special attention to the areas highlighted by your responses and take onboard the tips and techniques—these will help you to reduce the number of A responses, next time around, and help you to achieve a more balanced mixture of Bs and Cs. After you have read the book and had a chance to put the techniques into practice, take the quiz again. Provided that you have answered honestly, you will able to directly measure your progress and should see a big improvement.

# Prepare For Your Customers

Successful salespeople concentrate on their customers: they are determined to make sales, but equally determined to produce a high level of customer satisfaction. To help you prepare for your customers in a confident, effective, and professional manner, this chapter shows you how to:

- Understand the relationship between a customer and an effective salesperson
- Make a strong first impression by looking professional and having the right attitude
- Communicate persuasively, understand when to listen, and ask the right questions
- Identify the customer benefits of your product.

# Understand the Sales Relationship

Selling creates a personal relationship between the salesperson and a customer. An effective sales relationship involves taking orders for products that satisfy or delight your customers.

## Aim for Customer Satisfaction

An organization's most effective salespeople are its customers. A satisfied customer who talks enthusiastically to friends and acquaintances generates new business. Many successful restaurants, for example, rely entirely on word-of-mouth recommendations.

A successful sale has three winners: the salesperson who made the sale, the customer who receives the benefits of the product or service purchased, and the selling organization, which gains both sales revenue and a satisfied customer.

> A satisfied customer is also your most effective advocate

## Create Relationships

Making repeat sales to an existing customer is usually quicker and cheaper than finding a new prospect and securing the first sale—so repeat sales are also more profitable. The customer-salesperson relationship is a vital element in winning repeat sales. It is based on mutual confidence: customers reveal information about their needs and wants, or their company's problems and opportunities. In return, the salesperson maintains confidentiality and helps the customer to buy products that meet those requirements. You can build relationships by concentrating on providing your customers with solutions that produce real benefits.

---

**TIP** Strive to meet, and if possible exceed, your customer's expectations—or as many successful salespeople put it, "under-promise and over-perform."

## Observe Other Salespeople

**You can learn a lot about good—and bad—salesmanship by observing how other salespeople treat their customers. Examples of different sales techniques are all around you.**

Next time you are in a store or restaurant, take a moment to study the people working there and note how they interact with customers.

→ Can you identify any particularly effective salespeople? What are their sales techniques? Are they pushy? Professional?
→ What kind of relationship does a successful salesperson create with his or her customers? Look for ways in which the salesperson seeks to create a sense of trust.
→ Are there any approaches that elicit a negative response from a customer? How did the salesperson respond?

You can also use your own experiences to help you to understand and appreciate different sales techniques: next time someone tries to sell you something, pay close attention to the methods used.

→ What did the salesperson do that made you feel ready to buy?
→ Was the salesperson good at finding out what you wanted?
→ Did the product live up to the salesperson's promise?
→ Was the salesperson helpful in making sure that you got good after-sales service?
→ Was there anything the salesperson said or did that made you feel less inclined to buy?

### Effective Sales Techniques

**HIGH IMPACT**
- Being friendly and professional
- Finding out exactly what the customer wants
- Absorbing and responding positively to customer feedback
- Being prepared to negotiate

**NEGATIVE IMPACT**
- Being over-familiar or pushy
- Telling customers what you think they should want
- Ignoring customer feedback or becoming annoyed or aggressive
- Being inflexible

# Make a Good First Impression

Prospective customers, or prospects, like everyone else, make a rapid decision about a person they are meeting for the first time. It takes only a few seconds to make an impression, so make sure you prepare carefully.

## Look Professional

It is important to fit in with the customer's image of a person they enjoy talking to and working with. If you are selling to people who traditionally wear suits and ties, then dress accordingly; if you are a salesperson in a clothing boutique, you may be able to dress more casually. In all cases, however, the key is to look clean, neat, and polished. A professional appearance will ensure that your prospective customer takes you seriously from the start.

## Develop Confidence

Most salespeople feel some anxiety when they are new to the profession. The trick is to convert that energy into a more useful emotion. Keep a positive mental attitude—believe that you and your products and services can improve the businesses and lives of your customers. In a competitive position, this self-belief can be the difference between winning the order and losing out to a competitor.

> ### think SMART
>
> **To overcome any nerves you may feel when meeting a new prospect, and to appear more confident, simply pretend that you are meeting an old friend.**
>
> Imagine that the prospect is an old acquaintance that you haven't seen for many years. You are pleased to see the friend again and curious to find out what he or she has been up to since you last met. Adopt this attitude from the outset and the conversation should soon start to flow naturally.

## Make an Impact

A good upright stance, direct eye contact, and a firm handshake give an impression of confidence when you meet new prospects. A neat appearance and excellent manners ensure that you make a positive first impression.

**Posture** Stand upright but relaxed, and avoid hunching your shoulders or hanging your head. Do not cross your arms—this can look defensive.

**Handshake** Keep your palms angled slightly upward as you move to shake hands. Adopt a handshake that is firm, without being crushing.

**Eye contact** Make regular eye contact when talking or listening to indicate that you are honest and confident. Be careful not to stare.

**TIP Before meeting with potential customers, take a moment to think back over past successes—it will help you to feel much more confident.**

# Communicate Persuasively

**Professional salespeople are expert communicators. They use conversation to engage their prospective customers, determine their needs, and demonstrate how their products and services meet that need.**

## Ask the Right Questions

Effective salespeople ask questions to encourage prospects to talk freely about their aims, needs, and wants. From their answers, salespeople learn where their products could be appropriate. The way you ask the question is important. Avoid closed questions that require a simple yes or no answer—it is usually more effective to ask open questions that encourage people to talk about themselves and their companies in more detail.

- Closed questions often start with words such as "do," "is," and "are." "Are you looking for new suppliers?" invites a simple response: "No."
- Open questions begin with words such as "why," "how," "who," "what," and "where." "How can your suppliers offer you a better service?" opens up the conversation and can reveal useful information.

## TECHNIQUES *to* practice

**The ability to listen without interrupting is invaluable.** Practice your listening skills on a friend by asking an open question about a topic he or she is interested in; listen for two minutes without interrupting.

- Use nods and encouraging words to show that you are paying close attention.
- Subtly mirror the other person's posture and gestures to create empathy and rapport.
- Use silence to draw hesitant talkers into speaking.
- If conversation flags, ask more open questions—but make sure that the other person does most of the talking.
- Repeat key words silently as you listen to help you remember what is said.

## CASE study: Getting Customer Feedback

Carlos, a representative of a toy supplier, was having difficulty persuading a store manager, Eileen, to buy stocks of a new range of board games. Carlos's manager asked him how he usually started sales calls. She found that he always opened by describing the new range and showing the shop manager samples. She suggested Carlos first ask Eileen what type of products were currently selling well. Carlos did this, and picked up on the fact that board games for adults were selling well in her store that season. Carlos was able to use this knowledge to emphasize those features of his new range that would appeal to adults. Eileen bought stocks of the new range.

- *By finding out what kind of products were selling well before beginning his pitch, Carlos was better able to market his own product so that it matched the prospect's demands. He was able to respond as well as inform.*
- *The questions also established a two-way relationship between prospect and salesman. Instead of simply listening, Eileen felt that she'd made a contribution to the conversation and had an investment in the outcome.*

### Learn to Listen

As well as listening carefully while a prospect talks, you should also show that you are listening by looking attentive. If you miss something or do not understand what has been said, apologize and ask the customer to repeat the point. Active listening like this shows that you do not want to dominate the conversation.

- Pick up clues from what the prospect says to trigger the next set of logical questions, but never interrupt a prospect who is talking. Interrupting someone sends out a clear message: "What I want to say is more important than what you are trying to tell me."
- If a prospect asks you a question, keep your answers direct, positive, and to the point.

> **Unless one is a genius, it is best to aim at being intelligible.**
> Sir Anthony Hope Hopkins

## Talk in the Prospect's Terms

When you are selling, connect your product with something the prospect needs or wants. Describe that connection in words that the prospect uses rather than your own—he or she will relate to it more easily. When talking to a prospect, focus on the key words used and silently repeat them. Use these words when you respond.

## Aim to Close

Closed questions that require a "yes" or "no" tell you how close you are to a sale and ensure that you agree. Perhaps you want someone to attend a demonstration. Ask a direct closed question: "Will you personally attend?" If your prospect says "no," ask why and deal with the objection. A "yes" indicates that you have gotten a commitment to a course of action. If the prospect is wavering, refer to other benefits that have not previously been discussed; this may prove persuasive.

**Customer Benefits** Describe your product in terms of what your prospect needs or wants. If your prospect is looking for a family car, for example, you might want to emphasize trunk space and safety features rather than acceleration.

## Learn Your Customer's Jargon

**Every industry has its own jargon. To make sure you communicate effectively with customers and prospects, you need to be able to use their jargon with confidence.**

Jargon serves a dual purpose; it both aids communication and signals inclusion within a specific group or profession. If you can use your customer's jargon appropriately, it is easier to come across as an industry insider who understands the customer's needs and concerns. Inappropriate use of terminology can have the opposite effect. Confident and appropriate use of jargon relies on familiarity. Consider the following steps to develop this skill:

→ Speak in your customer's language, not your own: a computer salesperson who is selling products to the PR industry, for example, should avoid confusing less technically minded prospects with computer-related jargon.
→ Listen to people in the industry talking to each other and note how your customers describe their products. Curtain manufacturers, for example, call the length of a curtain "the drop." Identify any acronyms used—telephone experts often use the term POTS for "plain old telephone service."
→ Attend or read about industry conferences to find out about the key people—everyone in the industry knows the name of the chief executive of the largest company in the business.
→ Read the business section of a newspaper to find out about current problems and opportunities in the industry. Is it growing or declining? What are the latest buzzwords?
→ Visit all parts of an existing customer's business—even those that are not closely involved with your products. After all, it is still useful to know the jargon used by a different department.

**TIP Familiarize yourself with the key issues in the relevant industry so you can hold knowledgeable conversations with your customers.**

# Identify Customer Benefits
**Although your product may offer many attractive features, remember that your customers will only purchase what they feel they need or will use.**

## Convert Features into Benefits

It is not the features that sell your product—it is the benefits those features bring to your customers. All products have certain features that differentiate them from competitive products. A telephone salesperson, for example, may be selling a product that can retrieve voice messages remotely. This is a feature of the product—but unless your prospective customers believe that they will actually use this feature, it is unlikely to convince them of the product's benefits. Salespeople make a sale when they are able to show the value of the feature to the prospect. For example, an organization could use the remote access feature mentioned previously to reduce the number of times that maintenance engineers need to return to base. The benefit to the company is higher productivity.

Remember that the switch from feature to benefit can be a very personal one. A person may buy new clothes, for example, so that they look more fashionable—try to identify and focus on the benefits that are particular to each individual prospect that you talk to.

### Use "So What?" to define a benefit

**Feature**
The transformer breaks into two parts for transportation

SO WHAT?
⇩

When the pieces are on the truck, they are not wide loads

SO WHAT?
⇩

Drivers do not need a police escort in transit

SO WHAT?
⇩

**Benefit**
This saves on charges for such an escort

**TIP** Check that your prospect agrees with you that a certain feature is a benefit. If not, you may need to take a different approach to promoting your product.

## Make a Business Case

Large organizations use a business process to analyze the cost and benefits of spending money. There may be a purchasing department responsible for buying the raw materials that manufacturers use to make their own products or the items that retailers will stock in their stores. Line managers have budgets to spend on products that improve their efficiency or the service they offer to customers. All of these people have to look at the financial implications of a buying decision. Retailers will check on the profit margin of a particular line, for example. In other organizations, managers will want to establish the financial return before they invest in technology. Professional salespeople help a customer through the buying process and suggest financial benefits that they may not anticipate.

### Key Questions to Ask About Your Product

Just as large organizations will use a business process to analyze the financial and other benefits of introducing a product or service, you, too, need to ask yourself a series of questions to evaluate potential benefits and drawbacks for the customer.

→ Will the product or service significantly increase the customer's own sales revenues?
→ What current costs will the customer be able to cut?
→ How long will the customer need in order to recoup the purchasing or startup costs?
→ Are there any extra costs the customer would incur by not introducing the product?
→ What additional management control does the product offer?

# Find Your Customers

The job of a salesperson is to find prospective buyers and turn them into customers. To do this well, it is vital to know how your products fit the market, and it is important to appreciate the basic principles of your customers' business. This section shows you how to lay the foundations for successful sales by:

- Determining your target market and relating your product to this market effectively
- Accumulating knowledge about your target market and identifying which people and organizations are your best prospects
- Making efficient use of your prospecting time through planning and forecasting
- Prospecting for potential customers and creating interest in your product.

# Know Your Market

**The better you know your prospects and understand how their businesses operate, the easier it will be to interest them in the potential of your products.**

## Understand Business Principles

Devote time regularly to developing your knowledge of how business organizations operate. Try using short, formal courses, CD-ROMs, and Internet courses, as well as reading general management and business books. Broaden your knowledge base informally as well. Talk to the business people you meet and ask questions about their organizations; ask store owners how their business is progressing; and learn from people in your own organization. Read the financial pages at least once a week—if you find them difficult to understand, ask someone in your finance department if they can help you improve your skills.

> **The basis for sales success is a thorough understanding of the market**

## Understand Consumer Markets

If you are selling to consumers, you will need to collect marketing information about your prospective customers. Your own organization may be able to supply some information, and market reports can also be found on the Internet. It is important that you do your own research as well. If your territory is a residential subdivision, for example, try to work out what type of households have bought your product previously. This will give you the information you need to target that type. Build up a customer profile detailing factors such as the sex, age, income, and lifestyle of your target customers.

---

**TIP** **Identify the key decision-makers within target groups or organizations and find out what they want.**

## Understand Corporate Markets

If you are selling to a particular industry, get to know it as thoroughly as possible. Build up company profiles of target customers, based on factors such as size and turnover. Ask an existing customer to show you around the organization or explain how it operates. Read the trade press so that you are as well-informed on the industry as your customers.

Take an organization that you believe is a potential customer, then analyze the various divisions to find out which ones are most able and willing to spend money:

- Discover which of the division's activities are strategic to the organization—managers will spend money only on divisions that feature in their long-term plans.
- Check with any of your current contacts which divisions are growing or declining—organizations usually invest money in growth areas.
- Research a division's profits by reading the organization's published reports or checking newspaper archives on the Internet—profitable divisions will usually invest for growth, while less profitable ones will spend only in order to save costs.
- Check whether one of your competitors is active in the division with a significant market share—it is much easier to get into a division if there is no competition or if it is fragmented.

**Analyze an Organization**

Find out which divisions are growing or declining

⇩

Find out which divisions are strategic to the organization

⇩

Find out how profitable a division is (read published reports or check newspaper archives)

⇩

Find out whether you have a competitor in the division, especially one with a commanding market share

## Know Your Products

Your customers will expect you to have a thorough knowledge of your own products. As well as reading the relevant product literature, it is also helpful to study your products from the user's point of view. If it is feasible to try the products yourself, then you will be able to ensure that you are totally familiar with their features and operation. After all, someone who sells software for personal computers should also be a confident user of that software to be able to advise customers on any practical issues and questions they may have. Remember, though, that you are selling not the features of the product but the benefits they bring to your customers.

## Relate Products to a Market

It is important to identify the fit between your products and their potential markets. Bear in mind that a product is a useful part of your portfolio only if you can identify a market for it; while the only markets worth prospecting are those for which you have a suitable product. A restaurant that is surrounded by offices and near a high-end residential subdivision, for example, has at least two distinct markets. The food it offers at lunchtime should be appropriate for busy office staff who want to eat with their colleagues and get back to work. The food it sells in the evening should be appropriate for people who want to enjoy a leisurely dinner with family and friends. If the restaurant tries to sell the same food or maintain the same level of service throughout the day, it may find itself without a product/market fit.

> **Think of your products solely in terms of customer benefits**

**TIP** **Explore the benefits and shortcomings of your competitor's products as well as your own.**

## Group Products and Services

**A simple product/market matrix will help you to match your products or services with their most suitable markets, and prioritize the time you spend prospecting.**

Draw up a matrix with your products down one side and the target markets along the top. This will help you to clarify the fit between each product and its potential consumers. It will also help you to decide how much time and effort you should invest in prospecting the different areas.

→ If you offer many different products or services, you may need to sort them into groups. Choose criteria that seem appropriate to the markets, such as price, or whether service provision is easy or complex.

→ Sort target markets into groups depending on the relevant product criteria—into large or small organizations, for example, or into lunchtime and evening trade.

→ Recognize that markets change and revisit the prospecting matrix from time to time to make sure it is still appropriate. Change the level of activity where necessary, and discipline yourself to work according to this logical plan.

### Product/Market Groupings

|  | Market 1 | Market 2 | Market 3 |
|---|---|---|---|
| **Product 1** | High prospecting activity | Low prospecting activity | Medium prospecting activity |
| **Product 2** | Not applicable | Low prospecting activity | Medium prospecting activity |
| **Product 3** | High prospecting activity | Not applicable | High prospecting activity |
| **Product 4** | Low prospecting activity | High prospecting activity | High prospecting activity |

KNOW YOUR MARKET

## Get Organized
**To be successful in selling, you must be well-organized. You should also have a procedure for capturing data about prospects and customers, and you need to be able to manage your time effectively.**

### Build a Lifetime Address Book
As a professional salesperson, it is vital that you maintain contact with as many people as possible. People's requirements change, as will your products and services. Someone with whom you did not do business at your first attempt may become a good prospect at a later date. Both you and your contacts will also change organizations from time to time. Someone that you worked with in your previous organization could become a prospect for your current products. Collect data about everyone you know, business and personal, and keep it in your lifetime address book. Whether you do this electronically or manually, you must be able to take it with you when you move to another organization.

### Plan Your Week
For most salespeople, any selling week will consist of various elements, including visiting prospects and customers; administrative work, such as preparing proposals and quotations; internal meetings;

#### 5 minute FIX
**If you need to make lots of contacts over a short period of time, try limiting the details you note down to an email and phone number.**

- Business and personal email addresses tend to stay correct for longer than physical addresses.
- Cell phone numbers often have a longer life span than landline numbers.

> **If you are failing to plan, you are planning to fail.**
> Tariq Siddique

FIND YOUR CUSTOMERS

**TIP** **Vary the days and times spent prospecting—it may be impossible to contact a particular person at a certain time of day because of their schedule.**

research; and self-development work. List these activities, decide how much time per week you will allocate to them, and plan a typical weekly schedule. Include regular blocks of time for activities you are likely to put off, such as prospecting. It pays to set demanding targets—a daily target might comprise four sales, four quotations, and one hour devoted to finding at least four new prospects.

**Lifetime Contact Book** Whether you store your contacts manually or electronically, you must be able to take the data with you if you move to another organization. It is also vital to back up electronic data in a more stable form.

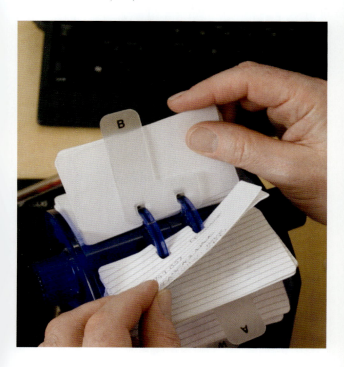

GET ORGANIZED 31

# The Sales Forecast
**An accurate sales forecast is an essential planning tool in any organization. It is used as the basis for many other projections, such as production and distribution plans.**

## Set Targets
Whatever product or service you are trying to sell, a good sales forecast will help you to plan for the future. Sales forecasting begins with your sales target. Your manager may have set a level of business for you to achieve during the financial year. You may also be asked to achieve certain other targets, such as monthly or quarterly ones, as well as sales to new customers. Alternatively, you may have targets that you have set yourself. Expect these targets to be demanding in today's competitive world. By comparing these targets to your forecast sales, you will get a clearer sense of whether the targets are realistic, and whether or not you are currently on track. Break down your target into appropriate sections so that you can measure your progress as the year proceeds—it can be difficult to catch up if you fall behind significantly.

## Make a Forecast
The precise format of your sales forecast is likely to vary, depending on how many products or services you offer. However, it will probably comprise a spreadsheet, where the estimated number of sales for different products are broken down over the course of the month or year, together with the projected value of these sales. A good way to reach a realistic figure is to evaluate your chances of making each sale in terms of a percentage figure. Remember that the forecast does not need to be highly detailed or 100 percent accurate—it is an educated guess rather than an exact calculation.

---

**TIP Even when prospecting for new customers, always set aside time to take care of existing clients.**

## The Forecasting System

**This system ensures that you are making the best use of your time and have a realistic picture of expected sales.**

Think about a current sales campaign and ask yourself: "What are the chances that this customer or prospect will place an order for this value of sales revenue?" Make sure you respond honestly:

→ If a customer has already placed an order, there is a 100 percent chance factor you will receive that value of sales revenue.
→ If you have a letter of intent subject to contract, the likely sales revenue has a chance factor of 75 percent.
→ If the prospect is going to place the order with either you or a competitor, score the potential sales revenue at 50 percent.
→ In all other instances where there is a real chance the prospect will place an order for that value of revenue, it is 25 percent.
→ If you do not have enough information to calculate the likelihood of an order, keep them on the list but give the potential sales revenue a 0 percent chance factor.

In a new territory, you may start with only 0 percent chance factors.

### Example of a Sales Forecast

| Sales revenue | 100% chance factor | 75% chance factor | 50% chance factor | 25% chance factor | 0% chance factor |
|---|---|---|---|---|---|
| **Prospect 1** | $10,000 | $20,000 | $36,000 | $100,000 | $250,000 |
| **Prospect 2** | - | - | $40,000 | $90,000 | $100,000 |
| **Potential sales totals** | $10,000 | $20,000 | $76,000 | $190,000 | $350,000 |
| **Factor** | 1 | .75 | .5 | .25 | 0 |
| **Likely sales totals** | $10,000 | $15,000 | $38,000 | $47,500 | $0 |
| **Forecast total** | $110,500 | | | | |
| **Target** | $120,000 | | | | |
| **Shortfall** | $9,500 | | | | |

THE SALES FORECAST

# Find Your Prospects

**A prospective customer, or prospect, is a person or an organization that has expressed an interest in your product or service. The more prospects you can find, the more sales you are likely to make.**

## Create Interest

Encourage prospects to find you by drawing attention to your product or service. To create interest in a retail outlet, ensure that both the premises and the window display are as attractive as possible. Also consider handing out leaflets in the street. In business-to-business selling, use advertising and promotions in the appropriate trade press. Look for opportunities to supply stories to local and national media. Whatever technique you use, make sure it is easy for a prospect to contact you. If you use direct mail, for example, always include a reply-paid form.

## CASE study: Understanding Prospects

Adrian, a plastics salesman, wanted to create interest in a new method of production. He sent engineer managers in his target organizations a mailing that included, as a promotional novelty, a model car kit based on the new process. By getting the engineers to build the model, he hoped that they would then contact him for further information on the process. The results were disappointing and few prospects got in touch. Adrian talked to his head engineer, who suggested he send the model with a piece missing. This resulted in many calls pointing out the problem and asking for the missing piece. Adrian agreed to deliver it at a meeting and, as a result, soon filled his planner with prospect calls.

- *Adrian's head engineer had a good understanding of the type of people Adrian was targeting. He realized that the engineers were probably building the models but lacked any specific inducement to respond. Crucially, he also realized that most engineers would be unable to resist calling to point out a fault.*
- *Adrian learned to analyze the type of person his mailings were aimed at and built this knowledge into his future campaigns.*

## think SMART

**When you start making live sales calls, contact first the prospects that you feel are least likely to buy your product. Jumping in at the deep end in this way can provide invaluable experience.**

It is tempting to start telephone prospecting with your most likely prospects, but there is a better approach. If you first telephone those suspects whom you believe are unlikely to become customers, you will be able to use those calls to work out what to say and how to react to problems. Once you have mastered the technique, turn to your best prospects.

## Identify Suspects

A suspect is a person or organization that you believe has the potential to become a prospect. You will need to build up lists of these suspects if you are going to create a solid platform for your selling activities. As an example, suppose that you are planning to sell a range of educational toys for preschool children:

- First, think about the types of people or organizations that the toys would appeal to: in this case, your suspects are likely to be daycare centers and babysitters.
- Next, put together a list of potential contacts from local business directories and the internet. To make your sales approach as personal as possible, try to find out the name of the senior manager. If the manager's name does not appear in a relevant publication or on the business's web site, you may have to call to find out.
- Finally, group your lists of suspects both by product and by type of market. This helps you to begin the important process of evaluating which type of suspect is most likely to become a prospect. Make sure you keep thorough notes of all the contacts you make on the list—you will need them for future use and analysis.

## Make Contact

Whether you make initial contact by telephone, or by other methods such as direct mail or email, consider which one would be most time-effective. One of your best suspect groups is other people working in organizations where you already have existing customers. Ask if you can use their name as a reference—it can be effective to start a prospecting call by mentioning the name of a satisfied customer whom your suspect already knows.

## Using the Telephone

Telephone prospecting is an important selling skill. Phone conversations are generally easier to control than face-to-face meetings because they tend to be briefer and more businesslike. To ensure the right outcome, however, it is vital to be clear, concise, and know exactly what you want to achieve.

**Phone Sales** Work from a script to avoid getting sidetracked, and make a conscious effort to smile—put a mirror on your desk to check, if necessary. A smiling face encourages a friendly tone.

## TECHNIQUES *to* practice

**Performed correctly, phone prospecting is an efficient way to reach prospects.**
You can develop your technique through role-play. Ask colleagues or friends to act as prospects. Sit in different rooms, and get them to vary who answers the phone and how they react. This helps you to learn how to react to the prospect's initial response.

- Write down in advance the topics that you want to cover.
- Speak slowly and clearly to prevent misunderstandings.
- Ask people to repeat numbers and other key details, then repeat these back to them to double-check for accuracy.
- Record the calls so that you can listen to them and get feedback from your manager.

When you make your first direct contact with a suspect on the telephone, ensure that you have a clear objective in mind. You have to create interest in your product, of course, but you must also be sure of what you want to happen next. You may want to create enough interest in one telephone call to ask for a meeting with the suspect; or you may limit your objective to agreeing to send over some sales literature. Follow that up with another call.

- Start by greeting the suspect by name and then introduce yourself and your organization.
- If necessary, ask a question about the current situation to check that the person could become a prospect. Then introduce one major benefit of your product.
- If the person shows an interest in achieving that benefit, ask for agreement to proceed to the next stage.
- Take notes of what is being said so that you can summarize the progress that you have made, and any agreements you have come to, at the end of the call.

**TIP Endeavor to pay roughly equal attention to new and existing customers.**

## Effective Direct Mail

**HIGH IMPACT**
- Addressing each mailing to a named person
- Pilot-testing suspect groupings
- Changing mailing lists regularly
- Following up on mailing with a telephone call

**NEGATIVE IMPACT**
- Sending mail without checking if the suspect name is correct
- Sending badly targeted mailings
- Using an out-of-date mailing list
- Making it difficult for suspects to get in contact with you

## Send Out Direct Mail

Direct mail can be a highly effective and time-efficient way to find new prospects, publicize your products, or even sell your products directly. However, mass mailings that fail to reach suitable prospects or are thrown straight in the wastebasket as junk mail are a waste of resources. Try to ensure that your mail goes out to people where there is a strong possibility of a positive response, and make sure you address them to a specific person. Former customers and people who have inquired about your products in the past are a good place to start—existing customers are far more likely to respond to mailings than cold prospects. If you need to find new prospects, consider renting a suitable mailing list from a professional broker—this way you will be able to specify a particular customer profile.

## Possible Items to Include in Direct Mail

| ITEM | ADVANTAGES OF INCLUDING ITEM |
| --- | --- |
| Cover letter | Can clearly introduce main sales points |
| Flyer | More visual and colorful than a standard cover letter |
| Promotional DVD | People are always curious and may play it |
| Product sample | Allows the prospect to try out the product |
| Free gift | Creates impact; an incentive to open the mail |
| Money-off coupon | Offers an incentive to buy the product |
| Order form | If appropriate, can close the sale |

## Perfect Your Mailings

To develop the perfect mailing, you'll need to experiment. Send out a limited number on a weekly basis and keep a careful record of the results. Change just one element of the mailing at a time so that you can analyze what works best. Experiment with different lists to find the one with the highest number of replies, or the highest proportion of replies that became customers. Spend time on your opening line and on the benefits your customers will gain from buying your products. When you have completed the first draft, revisit it from the customer's point of view:
- Does the mailing make you excited about the product?
- Do you understand what the product will do for you?
- Does it say exactly what you have to do to proceed?

## Make Your Flyer Work

### FED UP WITH HAVING TO TUNE YOUR GUITAR?

Our revolutionary new range of guitars tune themselves. No fuss, no bother. Simply choose the chord pattern required from the internal memory and walk away—you don't even need to strum the strings.

The new self-tuning electric guitar

Please send me a copy of your brochure
Name
Address

Telephone           E-mail
Mail to: ABC Guitars, PO Box 123, Anytown, OH 34567-0123
CC189

**Headline** Most people simply scan the headline and stop reading, so use it to pose a question to encourage the recipient to continue reading.

**Body copy** This should present a clear, direct proposition—avoid making ideas too complex or trying to say too much.

**Photograph** This is the first element readers look at, so use it to promote the product and encourage recipients to read further.

**Coupon** Include a reply device so that readers can place an order or request more information. Code your coupon so that you know which mailings produce the best response.

# Summary: Targeting Prospects

Finding prospective customers is a key activity that lies at the heart of selling. The more prospects you can find—the more people who have expressed interest in your product or service—the better chance you have of increasing your sales. This summary encapsulates how you can go about finding them, and how to get prospects to come to you.

## Plan of Action

**1** Identify your product/market fit → **2** Create interest in your product

### Know Your Market

- Identify your product benefits
- Research your potential markets
- Identify the fit between your product benefits and their potential markets

### Promote Your Product

- Create interest by advertising and running promotions
- Ensure that you include clear contact details or an order form
- Ensure that systems are in place to handle the response

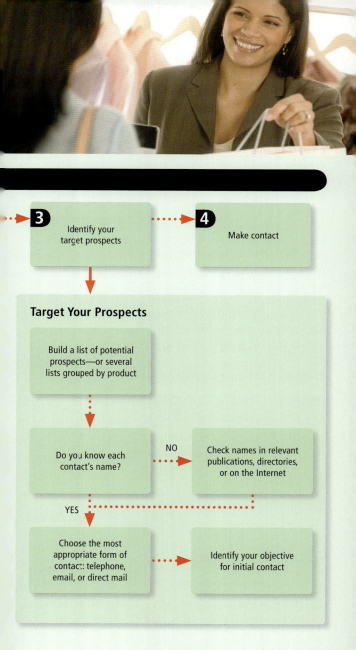

## Target Your Prospects

**3** Identify your target prospects

**4** Make contact

- Build a list of potential prospects—or several lists grouped by product
- Do you know each contact's name?
  - **NO** → Check names in relevant publications, directories, or on the Internet
  - **YES** → Choose the most appropriate form of contact: telephone, email, or direct mail → Identify your objective for initial contact

# Develop Your Sales Pipeline

**The biggest waste of a salesperson's time is time that is spent with prospects who fail to turn into customers. A properly developed sales pipeline will ensure that you have enough prospects to make your sales targets.**

## Learn From History

When you are actively talking to a prospect, you are conducting a sales campaign. Not all campaigns will result in firm orders, since the customer may decide not to buy, or to buy from a competitor. As a result, you'll need many more prospects than the actual sales you require to achieve your objectives. At some point in the campaign—provided you think there is a real chance of making a sale—you will need to present a proposal or a quotation. Aim for a high percentage of proposals to become orders. But again, in some cases, the prospect may not go ahead with your proposal, so you should make more proposals than you require sales. Keep good records of your prospecting and selling activity and work out your "conversion rate."

## Prospect–Customer Conversion Rates

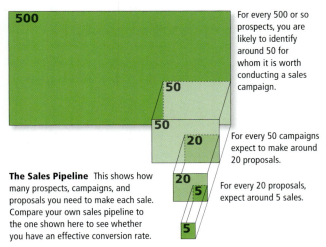

For every 500 or so prospects, you are likely to identify around 50 for whom it is worth conducting a sales campaign.

For every 50 campaigns expect to make around 20 proposals.

For every 20 proposals, expect around 5 sales.

**The Sales Pipeline** This shows how many prospects, campaigns, and proposals you need to make each sale. Compare your own sales pipeline to the one shown here to see whether you have an effective conversion rate.

## Plan to Improve

Analyzing your sales pipelines and conversion rates will help you to identify the weak points in your sales process. Try to learn more about the types of prospects who are likely to proceed from being interested to discussing the possibility of buying from you. Experiment with different tactics in sales campaigns, and use only those that give you greatest success. Play around with the wording of proposals and the way in which you present them, and identify which one is the most successful. Finally, use the sales pipeline analysis to find out how many prospects you need to make the required number of orders—and discipline yourself to do enough prospecting to keep your pipeline full.

**Customer profiling** If you can identify specific groups among your prospects, such as more mature women, who are particularly likely to become customers, you can target these groups right from the start of the sales process.

# 3
# Manage The Sales Process

In order to make a buying decision, prospective customers work through a series of steps until they feel ready to buy, emotionally and logically. The job of the salesperson is to help and guide the prospect through these steps. This chapter will show you how to get a prospect to the point of buying your product. Topics covered in this chapter include:

- How to plan and execute successful sales calls and meetings
- How to make strong, effective proposals
- How to distinguish good prospects and qualify out those who aren't suitable
- How to manage each step in the sales process, from opening the sale through to negotiating terms and clinching the deal.

# Define the Sales Process
**The length of time it takes to close a sale can vary considerably, but whatever the length of time involved, the steps in the process remain essentially the same.**

## Start the Sales Process
In some circumstances, you may aim to complete the sale at the first meeting; in more complex sales, it can take much longer—up to six months or more. But however long the process takes, the key to a smooth sale is preparation.

Before making contact with particular business customers, find out as much as you can about them. Use published reports, relevant reference books, and the Internet to identify:
- The products they sell and the markets they sell in
- Sales turnover and profit
- Their main competitors
- Business structure
- The key executives.

This should give useful clues as to which products might benefit them and what questions you need to ask your prospects when you meet them to uncover their needs and requirements.

### Understand the Sales Process

**Prepare**
Get all the information about the prospect that you need, and plan the opening call

**Open the sale**
Uncover the customer's needs and criteria, the people involved, and the financial position

**Build the sale**
Decide on the sales strategy, meet the key people, and present your solution

**Make a proposal**
Outline what the prospect should buy, the benefits, terms and conditions

**Close the sale**
Handle objections and take the order

---

**Every sale has five potential obstacles: no need, no money, no hurry, no desire, no trust.**   Zig Zaglar

## Summarize Your Position

**As you go through the sales process, measure your ongoing performance by giving each key areas a percentage score and recording your progress on a summary sheet.**

Continue to update this sheet as you move through the sales process. When all items score at or near 100 percent, the customer will be ready to buy. Key areas to consider are:

→ **Customer need** The impact and urgency of the requirement.
→ **Finances** This records whether the customer can justify the purchase and has the money available to buy it.
→ **Key people** How easy it is to meet all the key people.
→ **Time scale** When the customer is likely to buy.
→ **Solution** How well the product meets the customer's need.
→ **Basis of decision** How well the salesperson can meet the customer's buying criteria.
→ **Practicality** With complex products, how practical it will be for the customer to implement your solution.
→ **Competitive position** Whether you can persuade the customer not only to buy, but to buy from you rather than anyone else.

### Position Summary

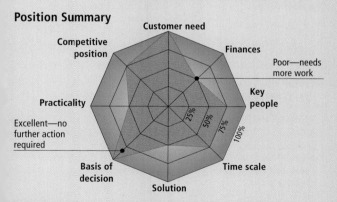

**Radar Diagram** You may find it helpful to record the results visually, so you can spot any patterns and can clearly see which areas need further work.

DEFINE THE SALES PROCESS

# Plan the Initial Sales Call

**In the relationship between salesperson and prospect, most of the power lies with the prospect—after all, they can decide whether or not to buy. You can moderate this advantage in one crucial way: by being better prepared.**

## Set Objectives

The first item to prepare in a call or meeting plan is your objective. This describes the situation you want to be in by the end of the meeting. Sometimes your objective will be to make a big step forward—such as, in a first call, to get the prospect to agree that you can present a written proposal. Sometimes they may be less far-reaching, such as getting the prospect to agree to your meeting another senior executive to discuss the issues. In all cases, they must be measurable—expressed in a way that leaves no doubt as to whether you have achieved them. Make your objectives as

## Sales-Call Meeting Plan

| Call objectives | |
|---|---|
| What are your measurable objectives for this call? | |
| **Organization** | **Contact and position** |
| Organization name | Name and position of contact Who are you meeting and what is the job title? |
| **Opening statement** | |
| What words will you use to turn the meeting to the business issue? | |
| **Possible objections** | **Counters** |
| What reasons might the customer have that would stop you from achieving your objectives? | How will you answer those objections? |
| **Sales aids** | **Customer reference** |
| What sales aids will you take in? (brochure, laptop, slide presentation, independent articles such as newspaper reports) | What satisfied customer could you use as a reference that your prospect might contact? |

**Sales Call Plan** Make sure you are well prepared and have all the essential information at your fingertips by writing down the structure of your call plan.

## TECHNIQUES *to practice*

**Role-play is an excellent way for you to improve your opening statement.** Ask a friend or colleague to act as the customer, and practice selling yourself and your services.

- Practice handling objections. You will be able to make a more confident and convincing response if you have practiced it before the actual meeting.
- If you feel that you have made a mistake, don't just start again—try to recover from it in the same way that you would if it were a real call.
- Ask for feedback on the way that you summarized and closed the call, then use this feedback to role-play your opening statement again so that you can perfect it.

far-reaching as possible, but also realistic—do not expect, for example, to convince someone to make a large capital investment in just one meeting.

## Plan Openings

Just as the first impression you make on a prospect is important, so is the way you turn the meeting from normal day-to-day conversation to the business in hand. Rehearse this thoroughly so that you appear confident and sure of your direction. Any hesitation here tends to hand control to the prospect. Your opening will explain why you are there in a way that gains the prospect's respect. If the meeting is one of a series, the best opening might be to summarize the situation to date before suggesting the business of this meeting. In an opening call, you might refer the prospect to the benefits that a customer has had from your products and services. Always finish your opening with an open question to get the person talking.

**TIP** **Take back control of a call by summarizing the meeting so far and asking the prospect a question.**

## Open the Sale
**During the crucial first sales call or meeting, you have two main aims: to excite the customer so that they want to move to the next step, and to make sure that the time you will have to put into the sale is worthwhile.**

### Agree on the Agenda
Start by agreeing on the agenda. Include the areas where you will be seeking information—these include:
- Understanding the prospect's requirements
- Finding out the criteria that the prospect uses to judge your proposals and those of your competitors
- Both sides deciding that it is worth taking the matter further
- Agreeing on the process that you and the prospect will go through to come to a decision
- Agreeing on the time scale for the sales campaign.

Emphasize the break in the agenda that allows both parties to reflect on whether or not to continue with the meeting and the sales process. If, having listened to the prospect's requirements and basis of decision, you believe that there is little chance that you can make a sale, it is much better to agree this amicably at this point. If the prospect actively agrees to continue with the meeting, this is evidence of commitment.

## think SMART

**Don't be afraid to ask your customers challenging questions. You might even find that the prospect starts trying to sell themselves to you.**

Try to ask questions that people do not expect from a salesperson. At the beginning of a meeting, for example, ask customers why they agreed to see you. It can be revealing to ask a challenging question early on, and often leads to interesting insights into the person's thought processes.

## Effective Openings

**HIGH IMPACT**
- Showing familiarity with their organization and their products
- Congratulating them on their company's recent achievements
- Being professional and friendly to receptionists and assistants

**NEGATIVE IMPACT**
- Appearing to know nothing about their business
- Pretending to know about their business and being caught out
- Treating junior staff members as though they are not important

## Build Interest

The prospect has agreed to see you, so you can assume that there is already some interest in your product's perceived benefits. Build this interest during the opening call by assuring the prospect—simply and succinctly—that you can meet all requirements and that the prospect will achieve benefits from buying your products and services.

- Resist the temptation to go into too much detail about your product and its features. Focus on the prospect and establishing the prospect's needs, wants, and concerns.
- Answer any questions about your product positively and succinctly. If you don't know the answer, steer around the problem by answering with another question.
- Encourage discussion by quoting from a relevant publication such as the prospect's annual report. If you are trying to sell a corporate hospitality service, for example, and the prospect's annual report states that they do 80 percent of their business with existing clients, direct your questions to prompt details on how they provide service and look after their clients.
- Give brief examples of others who have bought your products, and describe the benefits that they have received. Ask the prospect whether similar benefits would be a help to them.

> **Successful people ask better questions—as a result, they get better answers.**
>
> Abigail Van Buren

## Recognize Your Prospect's Interest

Carefully observe your prospect's body language as you summarize the ways in which your products can meet their needs. It may reveal important clues as to the benefits that really interest them. Most people are polite and will use words that indicate interest, regardless of their feelings; however, body language will often betray their true thoughts.

**Interested** This prospect is leaning forward and resting her chin on her hand, suggesting that she is concentrating on and may be seriously considering your suggestions. Her eyes are alert and her face has a neutral expression.

**Receptive** Eye contact and note-taking are both very good signs. Look at the hint of a smile—this person wants to hear what you are saying.

**Defensive** This time the prospect has crossed her arms and is leaning away, demonstrating negativity. Her gaze rests elsewhere, suggesting either boredom or hostility. Ask for feedback about what is going wrong.

---

**TIP** **Always ask questions about needs, even if you already know the answers; follow up the meeting by writing or emailing a summary of these needs.**

## Establish Customer Needs

Without a real customer requirement, you do not have a sales campaign, so the first area of exploration in the opening call or meeting is to look for the customer's needs. Ask carefully considered questions to uncover these. Start with the current situation in the relevant area to find out how the customer operates without your product. Then probe further to find out any reasons there might be for changing current practice—this may reveal the actual need. If there is more than one need, continue to ask questions until you know all their requirements—then present your solution.

## Summarize Needs

To complete the "establishing need" phase, use a summary to suggest that your products and services can meet the need in a way that offers benefits to the prospect. If, for example, you are selling packaged training courses for maintenance engineers, your summary might include the following points:

> Establish, address, and summarize your customer's requirements

- The prospect organization needs to train 130 people, but cannot afford to have them away from work for a week because of the demand for their services.
- The engineers are willing to learn, but spare time is at a premium; however, they spend a lot of time in their cars and could use it to listen to a training CD or cassette.
- The prospect organization wants their managers to be involved in the training, perhaps by using a guide to help the engineers get the most out of the training.

The summary has connected a feature of the product—the fact that the course is available on CD—with a major need: a training course that won't restrict working hours or interfere with free time. Ask a closing question at the end to get some commitment from the prospect—"Is that a fair list of your requirements?"

## Establish the Basis for Decisions

Everyone is looking for something different from a product, even if they have the same basic need, such as a car. One person may specify that the car must be small enough for his son to park easily. Another person may need a car that can be delivered before a certain date. Identify your prospect's basis of decision by asking a question such as "What is important to you in choosing which product to buy?" Listen carefully to the reasons and then repeat them back to the prospect, asking a closed question such as, "Have I got that right?" to gain commitment. In a complex sale, confirm this basis of decision in writing.

## Agree on a Timetable for the Buying Process

The most scarce resource that professional salespeople manage is their own time. They are trying to get an order by a certain date and a sale, or delivery, by another—so they cannot afford to waste time with prospects that do

### Define Alternative Criteria

Customers often start off thinking that their main criteria is price—only later to regret buying the economy model. You can help them to consider their criteria more carefully by asking questions about their basis of decision in three separate areas:

→ **Financial** Customers may have a budget for the purchase, either because it is what they think they can afford, or because their organization has set a budget for the project.
→ **Functional** This more technical basis of decision includes matters such as ease of use and reliability, as well as certain features that the product must have.
→ **Practical** The customer may look at how straightforward it will be to use the new product or service. An important example of this in an organization is, "Will the people who have to use it be prepared to change from their old methods?"

> **TIP** Use basis-of-decision selling to distinguish yourself from salespeople who take a less customer-oriented approach to selling their products.

not ultimately buy. It is helpful to agree on a timetable for the buying process: not only does it document the intended time scale for both the buyer and the seller, but it also adds commitment from the prospect.

## Work Together

At the opening call or meeting, use the drafting of a timetable as an opportunity to work with the prospect on a plan. If you sell complex solutions that have long implementation time scales, such as installing a new computer system, then extend the buying timetable to include an outline implementation plan.

By agreeing to a timetable, you will also remove any possibility of future misunderstandings: the prospect will know exactly what the full sales campaign involves, and how much time needs to be allocated to it. Equally, timetabling ensures that the salesperson knows that the targets can be realistically met within that time-frame. Ensure that changes are agreed on by both parties and that all stakeholders remain informed of the alterations.

## Draft Project Plan

**Set a timetable** This should show the key events in the sales campaign and the time allocated to each stage

# Qualify Your Prospects

Right from the opening sales call, professional selling involves checking that there is a reasonable chance the prospect will become a customer. This process is called "qualifying the prospect."

## Investigate the Financial Angle

The first key qualifying area is finance. When you go to a real estate agency, one of the first questions you will be asked is "What is your budget?" Your answer will "qualify" you as a prospect for a certain type or value of property. Do the same in any sales situation. Find out as soon as possible about the prospect's expectation of cost. If it is significantly below the estimated cost of your product, then you may have to "qualify out" the prospect immediately—politely inform them that you cannot help. In a large organization, it can be more complex to qualify your prospect: finance may involve not only budget, but also a process that managers have to go through to spend this budget. This process is often policed by the finance department.

### Qualifying Out Using Breakeven Analysis

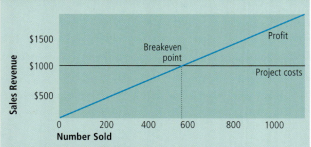

In this example, the salesperson is selling a project costing $1,000. The customer benefit is selling extra units of their products. The finance department has calculated that sales revenue will equal the project costs at 600 additional sales. The salesperson should qualify out if it becomes clear that the prospect does not believe that the increase in units will exceed 600.

## CASE study: Going Straight to the Top

Roger was a pharmaceutical sales rep selling products to a large hospital. However, the resident dispensing pharmacist showed no signs of buying the range, or of introducing Roger to the doctor who would actually prescribe the drug. So, without asking permission, Roger contacted the doctor directly. She was impressed by the product and subsequently instructed the pharmacist to place an order.

• *Roger realized that the doctor would have different purchasing criteria than the pharmacist. However, he also knew from experience that the pharmacist would refuse to introduce him to the doctor.*
• *By contacting the doctor directly, Roger was able to access the main decision-maker and gain a more authoritative relationship with the pharmacist.*

## Meet the Key People

The second key qualifying areas is access to the right people in the prospect's organization. You will have to work hard to meet the key people in an organization responsible for a buying decision. For example, your initial contact may try to dissuade you from meeting his or her boss, but if the boss is the decision-maker, it is vital that you do so. After all, the decision-maker's basis of decision may be totally different from your original contact's. This could mean that you lose the order because your products are not meeting the decision-maker's main criteria.

Deploy good arguments as to why you need to meet with all the key people in the organization—point out, for example, that you need to know exactly what they are all personally looking for; or that you want the key people to be involved at this stage because they will need to be involved in the project's implementation.

> **Spend lots of time talking to customers face to face. You'd be amazed how many companies don't listen to their customers.**
> Ross Perot

## Identify the Key Stakeholders

In some sales, a single person is responsible for making the buying decision; at other times, there is a buying team. If there are several team members involved, your campaign will need to address the concerns of each individual stakeholder in order to make a favorable impression.

→ In the opening call, ask your contact exactly who will be involved. Suggest that your contact provides you with an introduction to all the key stakeholders.

→ In a complex sale, particularly where new technology is involved, the buyer's team is likely to include several stakeholders, each with his or her own area of responsibility, whether this is financial, technical, or managerial. Angle your sales pitch toward the relevant area depending on who you are talking to.

→ Consider the example of a technology supplier who is proposing a major new system to an organization. The buyer's team includes the following stakeholders, each with his or her own area of responsibility.

**Decision-Maker**
This is the most senior member of the buying team. Aim to make your initial sales call or meeting with this person. If necessary, arrange a meeting between your senior managers and those of the prospect's to raise your level of contact.

**Financial Expert**
This person is responsible for vetting the business case for the investment. Present your cost/benefit analysis to this person.

**Technical Advisor**
This person confirms that the technology is suitable for the organization. Show how your product helps fulfill the company's aims.

**Functional Manager**
This person is in charge of implementing the system. You'll need to show how your proposed benefits can be achieved on the ground.

## Ways to Use Your Contacts Effectively

**HIGH IMPACT**
- Having easy access to all the key people in the buying team
- Talking to the top people in the buying organization
- Helping the prospect prepare a cost/benefit analysis

**NEGATIVE IMPACT**
- Having access only to the technical advisor
- Talking to buyers at a lower level than your competitors
- Avoiding talking to the prospect's financial people

## Use a Trial Close

The trial close is a powerful technique that will help you to qualify the prospect, measure progress, and find out what you have to do to get the business. It simply gives a condition and then asks a closed question: "If I could get it to you by Thursday, could you give the go-ahead now?" for example, or "If we can meet your buying criteria, will you go ahead with us?" Use the trial close frequently during your initial sales call to establish whether the prospect is serious and to expose any potential objections. Trial closing keeps the sales relationship friendly, while discouraging time-wasting.

## think SMART

**You could use a variation on the trial close to subtly check that you are not offering a level of service higher than the customer actually needs.**

For example, if you usually use an expensive courier service for delivery, it is worth checking if this is universally required: "If we get courier stock to you within two hours, would that make you feel happy to sign?" The customer may well respond that such speed is unnecessary. By not assuming that everyone needs fast delivery, you will have saved a significant amount of money and trouble.

# Complete the Opening Call

**The end of an opening sales call marks the beginning of a sales plan. Make sure you have all the information you need to build the plan, then finish on a positive note by highlighting the next steps.**

## Agree on an Action Plan

When you feel you have all the information you need, summarize what you have learned during the opening call. Almost certainly, one or two misunderstandings will be uncovered, so the summary offers the prospect an opportunity to fix them. Finish the summary with a closed question to gain agreement, such as "Is that a fair summary of our discussions?". If the prospect is in agreement, move on to the action plan. This will involve other people; agree that the prospect has an action to introduce you to people who are new to you either directly, or by a letter or email. Although most of the actions will be your responsibility, make sure the prospect has at least one action to complete to show an element of commitment.

## Check the Competition

Toward the end of an opening call, bring up the subject of competition. If you know there is competition involved, then you can use an open question, such as "How are our competitors doing?". If you have not yet established whether you have any competition, use a closed question

**5 minute FIX**

**Sometimes, after a sales call has ended, you may find you don't have all of the information you need.**

If you run out of time, or have failed to cover a vital issue, try one of the following solutions.

• Email the prospect with your conclusions to check that they're correct.

• Send a letter to the prospect enclosing a summary of the meeting and ask them to fill in any gaps in their reply.

• Ask someone else in the prospect's organization for the information you need.

## Essential Information for Sales Plans

| AREA | INFORMATION YOU SHOULD HAVE |
|---|---|
| Customer need | What the customer needs, the problem this causes, and the benefits of finding a solution |
| Finances | The available budget and the process of financial evaluation |
| Key people | The names of the key people involved in the decision and their roles |
| Time scale | A rough guide to when the customer will make a decision, and when you are expected to deliver products and services |
| Solution | An outline of what you are going to propose as a solution for the customer need |
| Basis of decision | How the customer will judge your proposal in terms of cost, functionality, and practicality |
| Practicality | A *prima facie* case that you and the customer can implement the solution |
| Competitive position | Knowledge of who the competitors are, the main reason they were brought in, and the stage they are at |

such as "Are you going to get any other suppliers involved?". This more subtle approach allows you to casually probe for information.

Some prospects will talk freely about competitors, so it is vital to probe in this area—after all, they will tell the competition about you. Other people are much more secretive about their activities with your competitors, but most will at least tell you what they perceive as the biggest advantage of each of the players. This is a good time to demonstrate complete confidence that you can not only take on the competition but also defeat them. Use a recent campaign that you or your organization won to illustrate your confidence. Look and sound as though you will relish the contest rather than fear it.

> **Make your products easier to buy than your competition or you will find your customers buying from them.**
> Mark Cuban

# Summary: Opening the Sale

First impressions make a lasting impact, and this is certainly true of the first sales call or meeting—how you well you can establish, summarize, and respond to each prospective customer's needs will decide whether this prospect becomes a customer. But the opening call also provides an opportunity for you to "qualify" the prospect: to check that they have the ability and the intention to make a purchase.

## Plan of Action

### 1 Establish Your Prospective Customer's Needs

### 3 Agree on an Action Plan

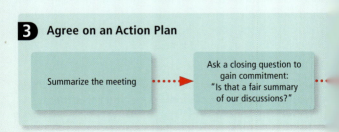

## 2  Qualify Your Prospect

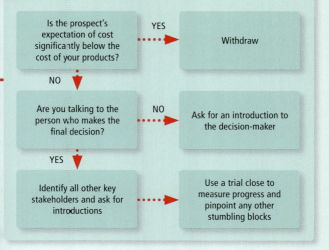

- Is the prospect's expectation of cost significantly below the cost of your products? — **YES** → Withdraw
- **NO** ↓
- Are you talking to the person who makes the final decision? — **NO** → Ask for an introduction to the decision-maker
- **YES** ↓
- Identify all other key stakeholders and ask for introductions → Use a trial close to measure progress and pinpoint any other stumbling blocks

- Ask about competitors, and show confidence that you can surpass them → Agree on the actions that you and the prospect need to take next

SUMMARY: OPENING THE SALE

# Build the Sale

**Once you have gathered the information you need by questioning the prospect, you will be in a position to set a sales strategy. Plan a methodical process to guide the prospect from being interested to being a customer.**

## Set Your Sales Strategy

A sales strategy is your route map to making a sale. Decide what you and the prospect must do to get them to the point of placing an order. This results in a list of actions that form the basis of the strategy. Beside each action put a milestone—what the action has to achieve. Then name someone who is responsible for achieving the milestone and the time target. It should be possible to set out the early part of the strategy in some detail after your first contact; later actions may emerge as the strategy unfolds.

**The Sales Process**

**Decide the action**
For example, a meeting of middle school science teachers

**Set the milestone**
For example, an agreement that they will use the materials

**Name the person responsible**
For example, the salesperson

**Set the time target**
For example, by October

## Use Demonstrations

Use demonstrations to build the sale. Make sure you get the right people to attend demonstrations. It's also useful to encourage the potential end-users to try the products out—their enthusiasm for the product will help to persuade the decision-maker. Rehearse demonstrations so that they run smoothly and professionally: a poor demonstration can harm your case as much as a good one will benefit it.

## Close In on Milestones

**As you set your strategy, remember that selling is a step-by-step process. Ensure that the prospect is happy with each step of the process before moving on to the next.**

A prospect will not make a purchasing decision until he or she has determined that the product is needed, meets the decision criteria, is affordable, and gives value for money. At each point, you must stimulate the prospect's emotional will to make the final decision:

→ Check that the prospect is satisfied at each stage—as you discuss each point, ask, "Are you happy to go ahead?"
→ If the prospect still has reservations, address these objections before trying to move on. You are both less likely to waste time if you know about an objection early on.

This process is known as "closing on milestones" and helps you to keep track of progress in a sales campaign. It also helps to alert you if your prospect is interested in a competitor's products or services: if a prospect says, "I was hoping it would have an automatic timer," this is probably because they have seen this feature on a competitive model.

**Touch and Explore** Encourage your prospects to physically handle your products and get a good feel for all their features.

## Identify the Unique Selling Proposition

Your product will probably have one or more unique features that are not available from competitors. However, a feature is only a unique selling proposition, or USP, if the customer needs it and can translate the feature into a benefit. Focus on the "value" that your proposition offers. If, for example, you are the market leader, the "value" may arise from your considerable experience in delivering and supporting the products you sell—your customers can therefore expect a smooth and risk-free implementation.

## Wait to Promote Your Organization

There are two key points during a sales campaign when it is appropriate to tell the prospect why he or she should choose your organization. The first is early on to prove your credibility as a reliable supplier. The second is when the prospect is close to making a decision. A prospect goes through a step-by-step process before making a decision:
- Do I need and want the product?
- Do I need and want it more than other similar products?
- Which organization should I buy from?

Time your "Why my organization" pitch to happen only when the prospect has reached stage three.

### think SMART

**Think beyond product differentiators when working out unique selling propositions—be creative.**

Your organization, customers, and after-sales service are all unique. Ask someone such as your company's owner or CEO to add value to your proposition—perhaps by offering your prospect a personal guarantee of customer satisfaction. Get a satisfied customer to write to your prospect. Or ask a relevant colleague, such as the maintenance manager, to explain how the prospect will benefit from superb after-sales service.

## CASE study: Countering a Competitive USP

Arun, owner of a small building company, was bidding to refurbish a neighborhood restaurant. However, during discussions, he realized that the prospect, Gilda, seemed to favor a competitor. He asked why, and she told him that the competitor's supply yard was based in the same town, while Arun's was 15 miles away. Gilda was concerned that the extra distance could delay her building work, should extra materials or tools be required. Arun decided to ask an existing customer, located more than 30 miles (50 km) away from his yard, to call Gilda and assure her that his project had never suffered delay due to the lack of materials or been compromised by distance. Gilda ultimately awarded the project to Arun.

- *By being proactive and asking questions, Arun was able to uncover Gilda's reservations and identify his competitor's USP—in this case, his location. This helped him re-pitch for the business in a way that dealt with the problem and even turned it to his advantage.*
- *By asking an existing customer—located considerably farther away from him than his prospect—to call, Arun added value to his proposition. Gilda felt reassured, and the value of the competitor's USP was undermined.*

### Create Empathy

Look for similarities between your organization and the activities of your prospect. Are you based in the same country or town? Are you of a similar size? Perhaps you are both addressing a similar market. Make strong openings to presentations or proposals by pointing out these similarities; this has the effect of creating empathy. People buy from people who understand the problems that they are trying to solve, so show your prospects that you can sympathize with them because you are facing the same challenges that they are facing.

**TIP** **The best time to try to sell your organization's benefits is when the prospect asks you the question, "Why should I buy from you?"**

BUILD THE SALE

# Make Your Proposal
At some point in a sales campaign, you must put your proposal in writing. Do this when you and the prospect have spent time working together. The written proposal should confirm what has been said.

## Write Your Proposal
The purpose of a written proposal or quotation is to confirm what you think the prospect should buy and what the benefits will be. It also states the terms and conditions of your offer to sell.

Make sure the proposal is as powerful as possible by stating the name of the person in the prospect's organization who has agreed with your statements. If, for example, you are selling replacement windows to the occupiers of a small office building, write down who has agreed that the heating bills will go down. Regardless of whether it is the facilities manager or the financial controller, the benefit will seem that much more persuasive if it has come from someone in the prospect's organization. Assign as many statements in this way as possible.

## TECHNIQUES *to* practice

**Keeping information short and to-the-point is a very useful skill to learn.**
To practice this skill, take an old proposal, a letter, or a magazine article, and try to halve its size.

1 Before you start cutting, make sure that you prioritize the facts and essential information.
2 Take out any irrelevant points, waffle, or repetition. These will only reduce the impact of what you are trying to say.
3 Go through each point and identify whether it is must know, should know, or nice to know. Keep the must-knows; the remaining points are not essential where space is tight.
4 Move the most important point to the front to grab the reader's interest.

## Structure Your Proposal

**The aim of a written proposal is to get a prospect to commit to a sale. To make sure that your proposal is as persuasive as possible, you should learn how to structure it effectively.**

Before you begin, make sure you have obtained all the information you need from the prospect, and have fully discussed the product or service you are selling and how it will be of benefit. Then use this seven-step process to structure your proposal:

→ **Background to the proposal**—this records the activities that you and the customer have done to get to this stage. It should display knowledge of the customer and its activities, mentioning the key people you have met.

> **The proposal is a written confirmation of agreements made so far**

→ **The customer requirement**—state the customer's requirement with an indication, if possible, of the cost of doing nothing. Try to reflect the urgency of the requirement.
→ **The Basis of Decision**—this section shows that you understand the criteria the prospect will use to make a decision to go ahead.
→ **Your proposal**—this is a simple statement in the prospect's terms of what you are proposing they buy. Avoid jargon.
→ **Benefits**—list these as the value the prospect will get from the purchase. Include, if possible, financial benefits as well as other less tangible ones. Where you are claiming that there are business benefits, you should name the person representing the customer who has agreed on them.
→ **Implementation plan**—this is a high-level statement of dates and key milestones in a complex project, or simple delivery dates if that is all that is required.
→ **Recommended action**—finally, recommend what action the prospect should take to accept the proposal.

MAKE YOUR PROPOSAL

# Present Your Sales Solution

**You will frequently be given opportunities to present your proposal to a decision-making committee or board. Make a big impression: a professional performance will secure not only this sale but also repeat orders.**

## Know Your Audience

The challenge of a final sales presentation is to meet the different needs of your audience, and these can range from the financial to the technical. Check who is attending, and what their interest is in your proposal, but tailor the presentation toward the decision-maker. If, for example, a technical expert asks a detailed question, check with the decision-maker if they would prefer you to handle that question outside the meeting. Look for signs of distraction: if the decision-maker appears to have lost interest, stop and ask what he or she would like to cover next.

## Structure and Timing

Always make sure that you keep to the time that has been agreed. Plan your timing to get to the Recommended Action item about three-fourths of the way through your allotted

**TIP** Use visual aids that are image-oriented and add extra value to your presentation.

### 5 minute FIX

**Effective presentations are targeted to the audience. So how should you react if you walk into the room and find more people there than you were expecting?**

- Find out who the new people are so that you can adjust your presentation.
- Get at least five minutes to make adjustments to your presentation by suggesting that they take a coffee break while you set up.
- Take out anything that might be controversial or boring to your new audience.
- Make sure the presentation still concentrates on the most important person in the decision-making process.

## Effective Ways to Present Your Solutions

**HIGH IMPACT**
- Using real examples from the organization's business
- Explaining the structure of your presentation and asking if they agree that it is appropriate
- Encouraging them to ask questions whenever they like

**NEGATIVE IMPACT**
- Spending too long describing your products
- Leaving them wondering what your presentation will include and how long it will take
- Making the audience feel that they should not interrupt you

---

time. If you have been given an hour, for example, try to obtain agreement to the next step after about 45 minutes. This leaves time for discussion and, if you achieve your objectives early, everyone will be delighted. Structure the presentation along the same lines as a proposal:

- Background to the proposal
- The customer requirement
- The Basis of Decision
- Your proposal
- Benefits
- Implementation plan
- Recommended action

> **Keep the focus of your presentation firmly on the customer**

## Deliver Succinctly

The enemy of a successful presentation is boredom, so watch your audience's reactions at all times. Make sure the talk is interesting and engagingly delivered, and remove anything that could be described as "padding."

- Keep the presentation short. Once you have achieved your objective, stop talking.
- Use a spoken-language style rather than a written one and try to vary the tone of your voice.
- Break the presentation up by using more than one type of visual aid, and move around—try starting your talk from a sitting position, then standing up to emphasize a point.

## think SMART

**Most prospects rightly assume that salespeople want to make presentations to them to win their business. Try a more subtle approach by asking customers to clarify what they are looking for from the presentation.**

If your prospects tell you that they already understand your proposal, ask them whether they agree that it would save time to place an order right away. This unusual questioning technique may win the order without a presentation, or it may clarify any objections that the buying team is likely to raise.

### Make a Confident Delivery

Customers buy from salespeople who appear confident that their proposed solution is right for them and represents good value for money. So a confident delivery is vital. You can gain confidence by rehearsing your presentation and ensuring that it has a confident and assertive opening. Suppose you are making a final presentation to a board of directors and your objective is to win the order; you can signal your confidence and intent by using an opening like this:

"Thank you for this opportunity to present our proposal. I intend to take an hour to:
- Give a brief overview of our proposal
- Ask if you are ready to go ahead with it
- Spend what time is left talking about delivery and implementation. Is that OK?"

This means that the audience is aware of your objective, and their response to your question will give you good clues as to how to pitch the presentation.

**TIP** **Make sure you can display your visual aids using technology available in the meeting room.**

## Allow Space for Discussion

Put yourself in the audience's shoes at a final presentation. They will find it difficult to make a committee decision while you are there. It is easier for the chairperson to thank you for your time and say that the committee will discuss it after the meeting. The chairperson will want to hear other people's views—but this delay means that they may not make a decision that day. Get around this by suggesting at the end of your presentation that you leave them alone for a few minutes before returning to find out their decision. This makes them feel relaxed, knowing that they can discuss your proposal among themselves, but keeps the pressure on them to make a decision that day.

**Make an impact** Visual aids can help to illustrate difficult concepts and make key points more memorable. Keep visual information simple and uncluttered and use bold colors that are easy to distinguish from a distance.

# Negotiate the Best Terms

**Toward the end of the selling process, you and your prospect will discuss the terms and conditions of the sale and negotiate a mutually acceptable deal. Make sure you negotiate hard for the best possible terms.**

## Identify the Issues

When you sell a gazebo, the prospect will be interested in several issues, such as quality and price. He or she may also try to negotiate free delivery and a time scale for erecting it. You can prepare for the negotiation by defining a specific objective, with tangible measures, for all the terms and conditions of sale. The price of the gazebo is a tangible measure, but you and the prospect also need to decide how to measure quality—perhaps the lumber can be further protected against the weather, for example. Make a list of all the issues involved in the negotiation, and work out your specific objectives and measures for each one.

## Set Your Objectives

The aim of a negotiation is to achieve agreement between both parties about how to proceed, and to resolve conflicting interests. Perhaps the prospect wants you—a kitchen supplier—to install the units using the same people who built them. You want them to use non-specialist installers to reduce costs and let the manufacturing side

### The Impact of Discounts

When negotiating on price, remember that even a small discount can have a massive impact on profitability. Take this example of an insurance salesperson who has been asked for a 10 percent discount:

| DEAL WITH NO DISCOUNT | | DEAL DISCOUNTED BY 10% | |
|---|---|---|---|
| Insurance premium | $1,000 | Discounted insurance premium | $900 |
| Cost of insurance | $800 | Cost of insurance | $800 |
| Gross profit | $200 | Gross profit | $100 |
| Expenses | $50 | Expenses | $50 |
| **Net profit** | **$150** | **Net profit** | **$50** |

## Build Negotiating Confidence

Prepare thoroughly for negotiations by thinking through all the issues that the prospect might raise and preparing your responses. This will help you to give a positive response to the concessions you anticipate they will demand. If you can discuss difficult issues confidently, you will place yourself in a stronger position.

→ Focus logically on an issue where there is disagreement—for example, the customer might want an extended warranty to be free while you want to charge for it.
→ Now give the customer reasons for accepting your terms—explain that it would be unfair to other customers if you varied your policy in one particular case.

Rehearse your response to possible objections in front of a mirror, taking careful note of your body language. Is it positive? Are you smiling where appropriate?

keep operating. Only make concessions that suit you best by assigning one of these three measures to each objective:
- The ideal outcome—the buyer contracts with another company to install the kitchen.
- An outcome that you will find acceptable—the lower-skilled unit builders will do the installation.
- An outcome that is the lowest you will accept—a production carpenter supervises lower-skilled installers.

The buyer can then be made aware that you will consider the negotiation a failure and walk away if they insist on getting your production carpenters to install the kitchen.

**TIP** **Practice saying "no" with a smile on your face; it will negate feelings of conflict during negotiations.**

## TECHNIQUES *to* practice

**The ability to keep calm during negotiations is an invaluable skill, in both business and personal life.** People will often betray their feelings during discussions or negotiations with friends and family. For example, they may show frustration if they are not getting their own way on which movie to watch, or when to leave a dinner party. If you can keep calm, you will not only strengthen your own position but you will also be better placed to guide proceedings to a more positive outcome.

**1** If you are feeling tense, take a slow, deep breath.

**2** Make sure your body language is relaxed and positive. Maintain eye contact, and keep your voice calm and your expression open and friendly. Try practicing this in front of a mirror.

**3** Be assertive and state your case clearly, but do not resort to aggression, intimidation, or emotional blackmail.

### Identify Needs and Wants

Be aware of the distinction between what your prospects want, and what they need. Imagine you are selling computer printers, for example, and your prospect needs a black-and-white printer for a business that has to send out printed documents. The prospect may also want the machine to operate as a color scanner for scanning in vacation photographs and sending them to friends. Separating needs from wants will strengthen your position in the negotiation. If, for example, the organization is paying, the prospect is more likely to satisfy the want; if the prospect's own money is on the line, you may have to sell the cheaper black-and-white range of printers.

**TIP** **Stay friendly but professional—being overly generous with concessions will not necessarily prompt the prospect to be equally generous in return.**

## Make and Receive Concessions

Make all propositions and concessions conditional—do not give anything away free. Giving any concession without getting one in return sets a dangerous precedent that a customer will exploit next time you are in a negotiation. It also means that the customer will feel certain that you can give more away: after all, if you can change the package in their favor and still have a deal that they find acceptable, how much more can they squeeze out of you? If a salesperson does this two or three times in a negotiation, the customer will start to suspect that the original deal was unfair and that the salesperson knows it. This creates resentment and puts future sales at risk.

## Set a Condition

Consider the following two approaches to making concessions, and note the different response each one appears to generate:

- "If you agree to pick up the product from our warehouse, we'll add the automatic timer for you, free of charge."
- "We could, I suppose, add the timer in."

In the first case, the prospect will consider how to get the product from the warehouse and may then concede. In the second, all the prospect needs to do is accept your concession and move on. If you then ask the prospect to pick up the goods, he or she may look for more concessions.

## Find a Compromise

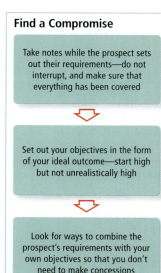

Take notes while the prospect sets out their requirements—do not interrupt, and make sure that everything has been covered

⇩

Set out your objectives in the form of your ideal outcome—start high but not unrealistically high

⇩

Look for ways to combine the prospect's requirements with your own objectives so that you don't need to make concessions

⇩

Make concessions reluctantly, and always use a conditional statement that seeks something in exchange

# Clinch the Deal
**The climax to any sales effort comes when you take the order. You can finish the selling job professionally by developing a good closing technique.**

## Close Effectively
If you think the time has come for the prospect to make a decision, use the summary close to guide him or her to a decision: simply summarize the situation and lead the prospect logically to the conclusion. Have the contract or order form in front of you, so that it's ready for a signature. If the prospect still seems reluctant to close the deal:

- Ask the prospect to list any objections, then make sure that the list is complete by using a trial close such as, "If I can answer all these points satisfactorily, will you then be able to place an order with us?"
- Answer the points, one by one. At the end of each point, ask whether your answer has been satisfactory.

When you get to the end of the list, if the prospect has no more objections, ask for the order again. Stay confident and friendly throughout, but be persistent—after all, closing business is why you are both there.

**Stay positive** Thank prospects warmly, whatever the outcome—if you leave on good terms, they'll be much more likely buy from you in the future.

## Handling Price Objections

Don't be discouraged if your prospect rejects your price outright. The prospect could simply be negotiating, so stand firm, remain professional, and take steps to explore the objections. Consider the following exchange:

→ **Prospect**: "I'm sorry, but your price is too high. I can get the same product 15 percent cheaper from a competitor."
→ **Salesperson**: "If we were offering our product at the same price, would you prefer to buy from us?"
→ **Prospect**: "Yes, I think I would."
→ **Salesperson**: "Why?"

At this point, the prospect may well list the advantages you have over the competitor—in effect, selling your proposal for you. If you hear that the prospect would favor a competitor even if the price was the same, ask "Why?" to uncover any other objections.

## Handle the Objections

When you have an uncommitted prospect, ask a closing question to discover why. Use the information to allay the prospect's concerns and get the sale. Practice by asking a closing question after each key step in the selling process:
- "So, you're looking for a tool to dig a four-foot trench but it needs to fit on your flatbed truck?"
- Then repeat these agreements to the prospect at a summary close to help guide him or her to a decision.

> **People get caught up in wonderful, eye-catching pitches, but they don't do enough to close the deal. It's not good if you don't make the sale.**
>
> Donald Trump

## Protect Your Time

Time is the salesperson's most valuable commodity. It is easily wasted on prospects who do not ultimately buy from you. Always react to warning signs: use closed questions and decide whether or not to withdraw.

### Ask Closed Questions

When a senior salesperson was asked why she was so successful, she replied, "Because, if I get a feeling that something is going wrong, I assume that it's true and act accordingly." Act on this. If you think that a prospect is not ready to buy, ask a closed question: "Are you implying that you are going to put off this decision until later?" Or get your manager to ask, if that is appropriate. Suppose you are selling training courses and suspect that the prospect favors the competition; give your manager a pretext to ask a closed question such as, "I know that you are still deciding, but I am just phoning to see whether I should provisionally allocate our trainers to your company for next month." Closed questions clarify the situation and assess your chances of winning the business.

## think SMART

**If you think a prospect is not going to be in a position to buy from you in the foreseeable future, you need to find out quickly to avoid wasting valuable time.**

Remember that prospects also guard their time jealously, and will not want to waste it if they do not intend to purchase from you. To find out if this is the case, ask a prospect to do something that—while reasonable—will take time or effort to carry out. Ask for information that requires research or ask to meet somewhere that will incur traveling expenses for the prospect. A refusal to act on such a request is a warning sign, and may be enough for you to decide to qualify them out.

### Avoiding Time-Wasters

**HIGH IMPACT**

- Regularly analyzing your position and checking that all your prospects are qualified
- Being disciplined in seeking and recognizing warning signals
- Making regular contact to check your prospect is still interested

**NEGATIVE IMPACT**

- Ignoring logical or emotional feelings that the campaign is not going to be successful
- Leaving closed questions until the end of the sales campaign
- Letting time pass and the prospect slip away

Sometimes a closed question can help you to identify whether a prospective customer lacks the authority to close a deal. If your prospect continually prevaricates and you are concerned that the deal is slipping, try a very hard question to probe his or her real intentions: "My manager has instructed me to pull out of this deal unless she hears from your manager that you are examining our proposal seriously." The prospect's reaction to such a direct approach should provide a good indication how likely you are to get the order.

## Qualifying Out

Avoid allowing a sales campaign to end by just giving up on it. If you have assessed the situation and decided that an active prospect is not going to go ahead at this time, qualify that prospect out proactively. Telephone and explain that you have decided not to take the matter further.

- If your analysis was correct, the prospect will appreciate your professionalism and be willing to work with you again if the situation changes.
- If you are mistaken, the prospect will explain why it is worth your time and effort to keep trying.

**TIP Consider making price concessions conditional on the prompt completion of the deal.**

# 4 Deliver Customer Satisfaction

The selling process does not end once you receive an order. The next goal is to deliver customer satisfaction. If your customers are delighted with the products they have bought, your opportunity for further sales is increased, and they may introduce you to other prospects. This chapter will help you to:

- Develop a customer-focused culture within your business or organization
- Understand consumer demands in retail
- Set customer service targets and measure customer satisfaction
- Handle customer complaints and put in place a first-class after-sales service.

## Put the Customer First
Although salespeople will be the initial point of contact with prospects and customers, the success of the entire organization depends on keeping its customers happy, and every staff member should play his or her role.

### Make Your Customers Visible
Everyone in an organization is engaged in some way with serving customers. Keep them aware that the real driver of their plans is the customer. If, for example, the support and administration people for your products and services are located on different floors, use a special notice board on these floors to display information about recent sales successes, and to keep them in touch with other customer-related points of interest:
- Ask your customers for feedback, and feature this feedback prominently on the noticeboard.
- Publicize any customers who have achieved something noteworthy using your products.

### TECHNIQUES *to* practice

**Learning to look at things from the customer's point of view will turn employees into more empathetic—and therefore more effective—salespeople.**
Learn how to promote the customer's viewpoint by using your employees' own experiences to make them think about customer focus. In any training course, ask them to think back to all the instances when they were the customers.

**1** Ask them to think of a time when they have been very satisfied as a customer, and to write down three elements of the supplier's performance that created satisfaction.
**2** Ask them to think of a time when they have not been satisfied, and to write down three contributory elements.
**3** List all their answers; ask them to suggest areas where your organization could improve its performance.

- Keep a file of newspaper clippings and magazine articles that mention your customers or products, and make the file accessible to all.

Selling is a team effort, so contribute to developing a customer-first culture. Always point out to your manager any changes or innovations in your activities that could improve service.

**Customer Care Board** Encourage team members to pin up information such as customer feedback, reports, and newspaper clippings on a prominently positioned noticeboard to draw attention to customer care issues.

### Improve Your Team's Customer Focus

Make a list of the tasks you and/or your team carry out

Decide which tasks have a direct impact on customers

Identify the benefit of those tasks that do impact on the customer

If the tasks have no benefits, change them until they do

## Satisfy Your Customers

**Your organization's image as a reliable supplier depends on the level of customer satisfaction that you achieve. Measure this thoroughly, and on a regular basis, to keep track of those areas which need improvement.**

### Set Customer Service Targets

Set high service targets and make a plan outlining how they will be achieved. Talk to customers about their hopes for after-sales service. Dissatisfaction arises when you do not meet your customers' expectations of service. Make sure you come to a mutual agreement about their expectations, and also that you can provide the level of service required. Consider all aspects of the after-sales service. Common target areas include:

- Availability of maintenance
- Call-out times
- Lead times for accessories and consumables
- Time scales for invoicing and payment
- Access to information.

Make your own list of the agreements you will need to make with your customers. Get into the habit of calling customers after a sale to check that they are satisfied.

*Good company reputations rely on meeting and exceeding expectations*

### Measure Customer Satisfaction

Find out whether or not you are meeting customers' expectations, by agreeing on individual targets for levels of service with them and then monitoring your success in achieving them. For more general feedback on customer service, use simple check sheets. For example, each time you make a delivery, ask the customer to rate, on a scale of 1–10, your organization's performance in these key areas:

- That the customer enjoys doing business with the members of your sales team
- That the product or service meets their expectations

## Use Managers to Assess Satisfaction

Getting everyone in your organization to start thinking about customer service is key to a successful operation. Ask your managers to take responsibility for a geographic area near their home or their base. Get them to meet those customers and ask a specific set of customer satisfaction questions:

→ Why did you buy the product or service?
→ How satisfied are you with it?
→ Would you buy from us again?
→ Would you recommend us to others?

This will enable them to obtain valuable information about customer satisfaction levels, which you can feed back to the sales, marketing, and after-sales service departments.

- That the administrative processes of ordering and payment are straightforward
- That your organization has carried out its commitments
- That your organization is responsive to customer demands for after-sales service.

Record the answers and look for trends in each area. Where an item is low or slipping, look for ways to improve. If you see a downward trend, go back to the customers who have marked the area lowest on their forms so that you can find out what needs to be done. When you have made improvements, call back those customers who had complaints so that they are made aware of your responsiveness. This may also help you to attract them back if you have lost them as a customer.

> **Glass, china, and reputation are easily cracked, and are never mended well.**
>
> Benjamin Franklin

SATISFY YOUR CUSTOMERS

## The Importance of After-Sales Support

Keep in contact with customers so that you can deal with problems before they cause disruption. In the scenario shown here, for example, delivery problems could reflect badly on the salesperson unless dealt with promptly.

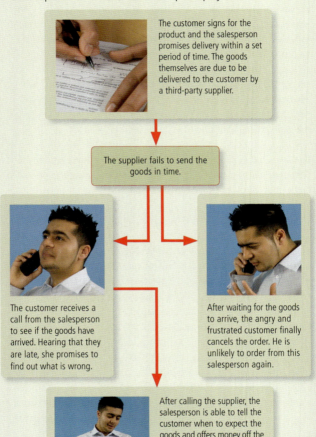

The customer signs for the product and the salesperson promises delivery within a set period of time. The goods themselves are due to be delivered to the customer by a third-party supplier.

The supplier fails to send the goods in time.

The customer receives a call from the salesperson to see if the goods have arrived. Hearing that they are late, she promises to find out what is wrong.

After waiting for the goods to arrive, the angry and frustrated customer finally cancels the order. He is unlikely to order from this salesperson again.

After calling the supplier, the salesperson is able to tell the customer when to expect the goods and offers money off the next order. Although the goods are late, the customer is happy with the after-sales service and places another order.

DELIVER CUSTOMER SATISFACTION

## Surveys

Further information can be obtained from customers by asking open survey questions. The difference between a closed survey and an open or qualitative one is in the phrasing of questions. A closed survey might ask:

- In terms of our after-sales service, are you very satisfied, satisfied, or dissatisfied?

Whereas a qualitative customer survey would ask:

- What do you think of our after-sales service?

Use an external organization to do at least some surveying—the customer is more likely to be objective with an outsider.

## 5 minute FIX

**If you introduce an entirely new product or service, you may need to quickly find out how satisfactory customers are finding it.**

A conventional survey may not produce results quickly enough. Instead, carry out your own short survey using team members or other salespeople to help.

- Take a representative sample of customers (up to 20 people or organizations) and call them with a list of questions.
- Use this feedback to identify and iron out any teething problems you may be facing.

## Focus Groups

Focus groups are another useful way to obtain information, although you may have to offer an incentive to get people to join. Make sure you have the appropriate people involved, such as sales and marketing, so that they can hear the reaction of the group first-hand. Invite between six and eight people so that you get a range of views and everyone has an opportunity to express their opinions. Remember, too, that you can learn a lot from focus groups talking to each other as well as to the facilitator.

**TIP** Be careful how you interpret a check sheet survey: "satisfied" usually means "not dissatisfied" rather than "delighted." Your goal is "very good."

SATISFY YOUR CUSTOMERS

# Satisfy Your Retail Customers

Retail, more than any other type of sales exchange, relies on creating an environment that helps customers decide to buy. An attractive-looking store invites a customer to enter, but the salesperson must go further to make a sale.

## Make Your Premises Attractive

Customers visiting a retail premises for the first time soon decide whether or not they are interested in buying there. To make a good first impression, ask yourself:

- Is it spotlessly clean? Customers are put off by hair on the salon floor, or restaurant tables covered in dirty dishes.
- Is it welcoming?
- Does the first thing they see on entering give a positive impression?
- Is the range of goods and services you supply immediately obvious?
- Do the colors attract the customers you want? Ask a color expert for guidance if necessary.

Always open your premises on time. If customers arrive and find that your premises are closed when your sign says it should be open, they will feel frustrated, go away, and possibly never return.

### 5 minute FIX

At times when your premises are particularly busy, it can be all too easy to let your standards of neatness drop.

Take quick action to keep your outlet looking professional:

- In a clothing store, if you don't have time to fold and put away all of the handled clothes, move those that are least likely to sell out of sight. Fold and bring them back as soon as there is a lull.

- In a restaurant where you are under pressure to clear the tables, ask new customers to stay at the entrance until you have cleared a table for them.

> **Give the public everything you can give them, keep the place as clean as you can keep it, keep it friendly.**
> Walt Disney

DELIVER CUSTOMER SATISFACTION

## Check Customer Need

**TIP** Store staff can never have too much product knowledge.

Avoid asking closed questions when making a sales approach. One of the most common—and ineffective—is "Can I help you?", which is almost inevitably answered with "No thanks, I'm just looking." Open questions establish need: if a customer is looking at armchairs, for example, ask if he or she wants a particular type. Find out the customer's price range and any other criteria that will influence the decision. When your questions have been fully answered, summarize your findings and guide the customer to the product that best meets his or her needs. Go to the top or just above the top price that has been suggested. Present the features of the product you are showing the customer and demonstrate how each feature meets each need. Check that the customer agrees that the product meets the requirement.

## CASE study: Getting Customer Feedback

Lee had set up a café bar in a small town. His target market was young professionals who worked in the nearby offices. He chose décor and furniture to appeal to people who wanted to go to a bar with some sophistication and flair. It was light and airy with chrome fixtures, pastel shades on the walls, and comfortable sofas. The feedback forms that he gave to every customer revealed that while they liked the ambience, they found the waiters' uniforms too formal. Lee scrapped the white-shirt-and-bow-tie uniforms and encouraged them to wear neat casual clothes.

- *By having a feedback mechanism in place, Lee discovered what his customers liked and disliked about their experience of his bar. He then made adjustments to reflect their stated preferences, making their visits more pleasurable, and making it more likely that they would return and recommend his bar to their friends and colleagues.*
- *Lee understood the importance of creating the right impression for his customers, even if it was not entirely to his own taste—he created an impression of what his customers expected to see.*

## Cross-Sell Your Products

Once customers have entered the store, you have an opportunity not only to sell them what they want, but to "cross-sell" other products. Effective cross-selling relies on identifying other products or services that add value to the customer's original purchase, rather than pushing them into buying unwanted extras. Done properly, therefore, it gives you the opportunity to guide the customer and improve the service you offer. Use open questions to establish further needs. Suppose a customer has just bought an expensive shirt. The closed question, "Do you also want to buy a tie?" risks a simple "No." But if you ask what sort of tie he was thinking of wearing with the shirt, you will make him think, and his answer will give you an opportunity to suggest a tie that fits his description.

Cross-selling works in any retail environment. In a bar, you might serve a drink and then inquire if the customer wants something to eat. In a travel agency, on the other hand, you may be able to cross-sell travel insurance.

> **Cross-selling expands the opportunities for customer satisfaction**

## think SMART

**If a customer wants to return a product, consider it an opportunity to win customer goodwill and build a good retail reputation.**

Losing a good retail reputation is easy, but winning goodwill and recommendations take time. Set your quality sights high. If a customer has a problem with a product—or even if they simply don't like it—take it back or fix the problem, without question. Encourage them to take something in exchange, but if they insist, always give them their money back. As a retailer, you are selling quality and service—not the product itself.

## Build a Database of Your Customers

Keep excellent customer records. Build information about your customers into a database and use it for sending out newsletters and other promotional material. Note their interests by recording previous purchases, or by inviting them to fill in a short form. Keep this to hand by the cash register. Then, when an existing customer comes in, you can not only easily access their record—saving time with the new transaction—but also suggest another purchase based on their buying history. A hair stylist, for example, might ask if the customer has enough of the conditioner that he or she normally uses.

**Cross-selling** Effective cross-selling requires some sort of relationship between the products concerned. If a customer has just bought a dress shirt, for example, ask what type of tie he plans to wear with the shirt and suggest a suitable tie from your range.

**TIP** **Promote your store by distributing flyers in the vicinity and talking to potential customers.**

# Offer a First-Class Service

Make sure that the service you offer your customers makes them feel important and well taken care of. Your organization needs to be responsive, service-oriented, and able to handle complaints professionally.

## Respond to Inquiries

An inquiry is not only an opportunity for a sale, it is also a chance to show how well your organization responds. The rule of professional salespeople is to respond to an inquiry within 24 hours. Be particularly careful with inquiries that come in via your website or by email: few inquirers through this medium get a response in 24 hours and a surprisingly large number get no response at all. When dealing with a key account, be prepared to send material to people who do not have buying authority—they can *still* contribute good or bad criticism to your reputation, and today's project manager could be tomorrow's production manager.

Remember that your response to an inquiry is often the first impression a prospect will get of you and your organization. Making a first-class impact at this stage

## think SMART

**Look at complaints in a positive light. They are often your best source of customer feedback and rather than being something to get upset about, provide a great opportunity to improve your services.**

Every company receives complaints; the most important thing is how you react to them. Once you have dealt with the complaint and reestablished customer satisfaction, look for the causes of the problem. There may be something wrong with the product itself, or even a flaw in the way your systems work. If you are able to establish how you can prevent it from occurring again, you will have also improved your service.

> **Your most unhappy customers are your greatest source of learning.**
> — Bill Gates

increases your chances of taking an order. Learn to produce a consistent template for action when handling complaints. Whenever you suggest a solution to a problem, always present your case with the customer in mind. Encourage other team members to use the same systematic approach to handling inquiries so that it becomes a common practice. Document the process so that they can refer to it. After a short time, they should start to use it automatically.

## Handling Complaints

Always welcome complaints. They are an opportunity to restore your relationship with a customer, find out what they really want, and improve your service. Customers who go to the trouble of complaining are usually interested in giving you an opportunity to put matters right.

If you then tackle the complaints effectively and ensure that customers are kept aware of your progress, you are demonstrating that you and your organization are genuinely sorry that the problem occurred. Even if the customer is at fault, avoid implying this—settle the problem and then address the issue that caused it.

## Deal with Problems

**Apologize**
Immediately take personal ownership of the problem

⇩

**Act quickly**
The rule of thumb is to act within five days

⇩

**Keep in contact**
Assure the customer that you are fixing the problem

⇩

**Deal with it**
Solve the problem, either in person or on the telephone

# 5

# Build Your Key Accounts

Your best customers are likely to produce a large proportion of your annual sales targets. Look after them professionally, and you should build a long-term relationship that will be of growing, mutual benefit—so aim to be involved in all aspects of your key account's work, including planning. This chapter will advise you how to:

- Identify the people in your organization whom you will need to get on board to help you get the best return from your key accounts
- Build a Key Account Plan to help you to make the best use of those resources
- Use the processes of Key Account Management to create a successful partnership.

# Focus on Your Best Customers
**Your objective as a salesperson is to apply your own time—and your organization's resources—to maximize return or productivity. Start by identifying your best customers and figuring out how to keep them.**

## Recognize Your Best Customers
Your best customers are those who will place the most orders for your products and services in a way that is both profitable and long-term. They will not necessarily be the customers with whom you currently do the most business. Imagine, for example, that you are selling advertising space in a gourmet dining magazine and that a famous chef opens up a new chain of restaurants. Although you are not currently doing business with the chef, the huge future potential means that he or she should be treated as one your "best" customers. Do not ignore major prospects simply because they do little business with you at present.

## Retain Long-term Customers
Selling your products and services to existing customers is more cost-effective than finding new customers. Stay up to date with events in your best customers' industries

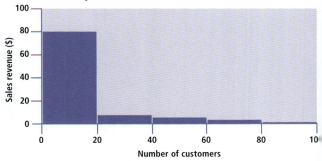

**The 80/20 Rule** This states that 80 percent of your sales revenue comes from just 20 percent of your customers. The exact figures will vary, but there's no doubt that your most profitable customers deserve a similarly high proportion of your time.

## Look for Trends

Your best customers are likely to be those operating in growth industries that show signs of maintaining that growth. To identify customers who will be most important to you in the future:

→ Look at the underlying trends in your customer's industry by using an industry-specific website or studying the reports and accounts of your customers and their competitors.
→ Be prepared to change your focus from one customer to another if, for example, one customer is increasing profits faster than another.

If, in examining the trends in the industry you currently sell to, you find that the industry is in decline, look at the practicalities of opening up prospects in another industry.

so that you can anticipate where new opportunities may arise for them—and by default, you. For example, suppose your best customer sells tires and exhaust systems and you have noticed publicity about a competitor who is planning a huge expansion of outlets on the outskirts of medium-size towns.

If you anticipate the impact that this will have on your customer, and take steps to find out what is being planned to counter the threat, then you will have the edge on your competitors. If, however, you avoid dealing with the issue until the new competitor arrives, you will be in no better situation than your competitors—even though you are an existing supplier. So you will have weakened your position.

**Identify your best customers and anticipate their future needs**

# Build Your Account Team

**If you are a salesperson or account manager responsible for key customers, persuade your organization to give you the resources you need to maximize profits from the account.**

## Identify Stakeholders

To secure the necessary resources, make sure that you identify all the people who have a stake in the success of your key accounts. There may be several stakeholders with a direct or indirect impact on how your organization develops its business with your key accounts. For example, marketing people will be interested in trends in your customer's industry, as well as future requirements. Similarly, the research and development people need to keep abreast of

### Possible Stakeholders and Their Roles

| STAKEHOLDER | THEIR ROLE IN YOUR KEY ACCOUNTS |
|---|---|
| Your manager | Meets with the customer regularly, perhaps at a more senior level than you. Represents your requirements for your customers to the rest of the organization. |
| Other account managers | These may be responsible on a geographic basis and will include salespeople working on the same customer account overseas. Responsible in their territory for sales and for carrying out the account strategy. |
| Maintenance manager | May meet with customers regularly, perhaps on a quarterly basis. Responsible for customer satisfaction targets. |
| Support manager | May meet with customers from time to time. Allocate resources to key accounts according to their priorities. |
| Maintenance engineers | Responsible for meeting service targets and for feeding back information to you about events at the account. |
| Production representative | Provider of products and services to your key accounts. Must be kept up-to-date with the account's changing requirements. Will also probably need to meet the customer occasionally. |
| Financial administrator | Responsible for correct billing and other administrative arrangements on your key account. May also advise the organization on the financial viability of your plans. |

**Role Play** Structured role play to explore the potential scenarios that can crop up with key account customers will help the different members of your sales team to focus more effectively on customer satisfaction.

your customer's requirements, along with any relevant information about competitive products. Before preparing a customer development plan, ensure that you have a complete list of these stakeholders and have agreed on their roles.

## Get Resources

Account managers do not have direct control over the resources—in this instance, people—that they want to apply to their accounts. You must therefore try to convince the appropriate managers to direct some of their resources to your accounts by developing a resource plan.

The resource plan should identify the return on the investment in your customer of these resources in terms of sales and profits. Form both the stakeholders and the resources into a "virtual" team who are engaged regularly, or from time to time, with your account.

**TIP Meet informally with stakeholders and team members, as well as formally, to discuss account progress.**

# Use the Key Account Process

**Manage your key account using an account management process to produce a key account. The plan's objective is to manage relationships, maintain satisfaction, and produce orders and revenue now and in the long term.**

## Know the Process

An Account Development Plan covers every aspect of your long-term relationship with your key account customer, and helps you to develop the "working partnership" that is your aim. Start the process with a complete analysis of the organization and characteristics. This will lead toward setting your goals in the account over the next year in detail, and over the next two or three years in outline. The goals cover the critical success factors of account management, as well as sales campaign goals, and aim to get the account environment into the best shape possible to support your selling activities.

Goal-setting leads toward an action plan that allows you to work out the resources you will need to implement your plan and achieve your objectives. As you implement it, review it regularly to ensure that you are developing a strong relationship with the key account and improving the environment—it will then present you with profitable opportunities and sales.

**Understand the Key Account Management Process**

Analyze the account

⇩

Set account goals

⇩

Create the action plan

⇩

Create the resource plan

⇩

Implement the plan

⇩

Review the plan

## Review Progress

From time to time, review your progress in the key areas. Record progress on a summary sheet and use it to inform the account's other stakeholders. The key areas are:

- **Level of contact**—Do you have access to the key people?
- **Customer satisfaction**—How well do you meet your targets?
- **Account planning**—How well developed is your plan and do you have the resources to implement it?
- **Competitive position**—Are you making progress or losing out to competitors?
- **Strategic areas**—Are you selling to areas that are strategic to the customer's overall success and are you aware of your customer's plans for moving forward?
- **Pipeline**—Do you have enough prospective sales to hit your sales targets?
- **Market share**—Is your share of the customer's business rising or falling?

## TECHNIQUES *to practice*

**If you are a key account manager, you must learn how to foster the total commitment of stakeholders and their resources to your own key account.**

Encourage this type of commitment in the future by showing your appreciation of any contribution they have made, large or small, to your success with that customer:

1 Speak to the key resources regularly to stay up to date with their activities and thank them for their help.
2 Send emails and notes to all those who have made a contribution, thanking them and copying in their manager.
3 Consider organizing an annual or quarterly award for exceptional contributions from your "virtual" team members.

**TIP** Always give the relevant managers advance notice of when you will need their resources (such as staff), so that they can plan to make them available.

# Critical Success Factors

**Develop your position in your key account with activities that concentrate on key areas for success. Improve the number and seniority of the key people in the account, and remember always to promote customer satisfaction.**

## Sell High, Sell Wide

In major organizations, a large number of diverse people can have a direct or indirect impact on your success in a key account. The benefits of having a wide range of contacts, preferably right to the top of the organization, are:
- That they will give you good access to the organization's future plans, helping you to identify future opportunities.
- That you will be in touch with people who are in a position to instruct people below them to buy from you, or will be able to bypass procedures that are holding you up.
- That they can safeguard you from being side-stepped by a competitor who is talking at a higher level than you.

### Broaden Your Contacts Base

If you do not have a broad range of contacts in your account, try holding a mini-conference on a topic related to your products and services. Ask someone who is not part of your organization to make a short presentation on the topic and take questions from the floor. Remember that the purpose of the meeting is to build a list of prospects and other significant contacts that you can use in subsequent sales campaigns. Do not treat it as a selling event.

→ Assure the recipients of your invitations that the purpose of the event is to inform—not sell.
→ Keep your promise and avoid pressuring anyone to talk about buying your products.
→ Have posters and handouts that feature suppliers other than your organization—exclude direct competitors.

# CASE study: Selling to Schools

Elena, a former teacher, was a stationery salesperson. She knew that local schools each had a budget for the types of products that she sold, so she made short presentations to teachers and administrators. Despite an excellent response, she did not get any orders. Realizing there was a problem, she contacted a colleague at her old school. He explained that while there was a budget at school level, all suppliers had to be on a "Preferred Supplier List" drawn up by the school district. Elena went to see them, presented her case, and was duly put on the list. Orders started coming in and she resolved to maintain a much wider level of contact in future.

- *By being proactive and making contact with a former colleague, Elena was able to establish that she was not talking to the people with the authority to buy. She then took steps to rectify the problem.*
- *Elena's initial ignorance of the system alerted her to the fact that she needed to widen her circle of contacts. She realized that this way she would be better informed and better placed to take advantage of any future opportunities.*

Make sure you cultivate a wide range of contacts by approaching all the divisions and departments in your key account to look for opportunities. Your contacts will then be more likely to approach you first, should they need your products and services in the future.

## Agree Customer Satisfaction Targets

If your customers are not completely satisfied with your performance, they will be unwilling to buy products or services from you in the future. Set performance targets, review these regularly, and address weaknesses as they appear. This is especially important when customers are locked in to your products and services: failure to monitor performance targets ensures that—because the orders continue to come in—dissatisfaction goes undetected. This builds resentment and virtually guarantees that customers will go elsewhere as soon as they are free to do so.

## think SMART

**If you are faced by a competitor in a key area of an account, divert their resources to an area in the account that is not your main target for the next sale.**

Suppose you want to make a sale in the Spare Parts department of a car manufacturer. Your competitor has a lot of business in the Production department. Simulate a major attack on Production by redirecting a limited amount of selling effort. The current supplier will then put extra effort in Production, leaving you free to sell in Spare Parts.

## Consider the Strategic Situation

When approaching an important account where you currently do little or no business, always try to break into the strategic heart of the organization. In a competitive situation, success tends to go to suppliers involved in those areas of the key account that the customer regards as strategically important. Imagine, for example, that you sell powder coating to a forge that makes gates and fences. The forge's main business, however, is shelving and other fixtures for warehouses and offices—so you are selling to a non-strategic division. However, your competitor working in the main businesses is already at the strategic heart of the organization, giving them access to top management and putting them in a stronger position. As a result, they will see an opportunity to replace you as the supplier. Realistically, you have two alternatives:

> Organizations spend more on areas they view as strategically important

- Maximize your efforts to get a foothold in the other business and eventually succeed.
- Reconsider whether this account deserves the special status of a key account.

> **You can make more friends in two months by becoming more interested in other people than you can in two years by trying to get people interested in you.**
> Dale Carnegie

## Make Sure Performance Meets Expectations

As a manager of a busy account that is buying and using a large number of your products and services, you will have to devote a significant amount of time to ensuring that your organization performs to expectations.

Ensure that you do not fall behind with prospecting for new sales in both your existing areas of activity and in new divisions that you have not yet penetrated. Check, too, that you have enough prospects to achieve success in your monthly, quarterly, and annual targets. And always balance the time you put into improving your long-term relationship with the basics of prospecting and selling.

## Analyze Your Market Share

A key account is like a market. Those parts of the organization to whom you have already sold represent your existing markets, while areas that you have not yet penetrated are new markets. Remember some basic marketing rules concerning market share: if your share of the overall market is increasing, your account is likely to continue growing; if it is declining, you run the risk that it will take a series of sudden drops. Work out your approximate market share and check the trend:

→ Ask your customer, or work out as accurately as you can, the annual total organization-wide budget for your types of products and services.
→ Calculate your share as a percentage of the total budget.
→ If possible, draw a graph of the trend over the last three years.

# Write Your Key Account Plan

**Drive the Key Account Plan from the customer's point of view by considering his or her strategy and current situation. This approach should help you to sell the most profitable mix of products and services.**

## Agree on the Customer Strategy

Start your account plan by identifying your customer's main aims. This may already appear as the organization's mission statement on its website, or in other published reports. Ask yourself, "What is the customer's purpose?" If, for example, the customer is a frozen food supplier, the mission statement might read:

- "To achieve a market share of 25 percent of the regional market for frozen desserts within five years by internal growth and acquisition."

In a large organization, your customer may have a number of divisions that have little in common. In such a case, consider producing account plans for each division.

If you cannot find the mission in the organization's published material, try speaking to senior managers and getting them to talk about their mission, aspirations, strengths, and weaknesses in achieving those goals. You should be able to glean useful information.

### Effective Ways to Plan Key Accounts

**HIGH IMPACT**

- Asking the customer to join the planning meeting and contribute to the SWOT analysis
- Checking a newspaper archive for articles about your customer to add to your SWOT analysis
- Checking the accuracy of your completed SWOT with a senior member of the organization

**NEGATIVE IMPACT**

- Making assumptions on the customer's position without real evidence
- Relying on the views of people who have not had recent experience of the account
- Keeping your analysis to yourself on the grounds that it is "confidential"

> **TIP** Keep the language used in the SWOT analysis simple, clear, and concise.

## Consider Strengths and Weaknesses

To ensure that your plan is driven by the customer's requirements, start your key account plan by performing an environmental analysis. To focus on the key areas, use the SWOT analysis technique. Ask yourself what the customer's strengths, weaknesses, opportunities, and threats are in terms of achieving its mission statement:

- **Strengths**—facts or events that are likely to assist your key customer in achieving its mission.
- **Weaknesses**—facts or events that are likely to hinder the customer from achieving its mission.
- **Opportunities**—things the customer could do to improve its ability to achieve its mission.
- **Threats**—potential disruptions to the customer's ability to achieve its mission and the eventual outcome of failing to address a known weakness.

Invite account stakeholders to a team meeting. Write the SWOT analysis on slides or flipcharts and list any areas of insufficient knowledge that you uncover on a flipchart titled "We do not know...". Plan actions to find the information you lack.

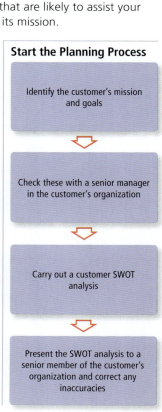

**Start the Planning Process**

Identify the customer's mission and goals

⇩

Check these with a senior manager in the customer's organization

⇩

Carry out a customer SWOT analysis

⇩

Present the SWOT analysis to a senior member of the customer's organization and correct any inaccuracies

## Agree on Your Aims

Begin the planning process by producing a short statement of your aims or purpose for your key account. Keep it broad at this stage: you will produce detailed objectives later on in the planning process. Examples include:
- To maintain our current level of business in divisions where we already do business, and to break into one new division in the next six months
- To become the dominant supplier to this customer, measured by market share
- To become the natural partner providing training courses in every division in the customer's organization.

The first two examples are clear and concrete. They avoid qualitative words like "be the best" or "highest quality" and will lead to a plan that is focused on actions. The third example includes the phrase

**Building relationships** You don't always need to meet your key account contacts in the office. To build more informal relationships, consider taking your contacts out to a restaurant or coffee shop.

"natural partner"; a definition of this must be agreed upon before continuing to ensure that the plan is concrete and action-oriented, rather than abstract and debate-oriented.

## Understand Your Current Position

Use SWOT analysis to examine your current position in the account. Be honest, particularly with your statements about weaknesses. For example, if team members lack skills in areas that are key to achieving your aims, document it so that you can agree on actions to fill those skills gaps later. When you have completed the first draft, examine the list relating to opportunities: as well as highlighting areas for making sales, it will also include actions you could take to eliminate weaknesses.

Try to find an opportunity to assist the customer in eliminating weaknesses in as many places as possible. Look for a strong link between your opportunities and the customer's weaknesses, opportunities, and threats to make sure that your action plan is aimed at producing customer benefits.

### Continue the Planning Process

- Identify your aim or purpose in regard to the account.
- Agree on these with your team by checking details with the appropriate people.
- Carry out a SWOT analysis to examine your current position in the account.
- Check that your opportunities address the customer's weaknesses, opportunities, and threats.

**TIP** During the planning session, make sure that everyone in the room has both an equal voice and an equal vote so that junior members can contribute.

## Account Management Objectives

**Improve your overall position in the account by assigning objectives to both yourself and your team. SWOT analysis will give you guidance: concentrate on the weakest areas.**

You will almost certainly need at least three objectives in every one of the areas listed in the chart below. In this example, the Critical Success Factors of professional account management are each allied to an appropriate sample objective.

### Writing Account Management Objectives

| CRITICAL FACTOR | POSSIBLE OBJECTIVE |
| --- | --- |
| Level of contact | To meet with each departmental manager to discuss strengths, weaknesses, and opportunities within three months |
| Customer satisfaction | To overcome the color-matching problem by agreeing on a standard color with the paint shop within one month |
| Account planning | To reconvene as a team to review the account plan after the visits to departmental managers within four months |
| Competitive position | To improve competitive position within the account by holding a joint planning session with at least three departments within nine months |
| Strategic customer areas | To receive an order of more than $90,000 from one of the key areas of Fitness Equipment or Kitchen Equipment within 12 months. |
| Key customer strategies | To improve our knowledge of the account's strategy by meeting with the group managing director to discuss the joint plans produced with departmental managers within 10 months. |
| Pipeline | To discover new prospects to the value of $230,000 within the next three months |
| Market share | To reverse current negative trend by replacing a competitor in Fitness Equipment or Kitchen Equipment within the next 12 months. |

**TIP** Work out a detailed estimate of exactly what resource you would need to achieve the target, then state the consequences of failing to meet the objective.

## Write Your Action and Resource Plans

List the actions needed to achieve the next 12 months' objectives. They will be clear in the short term and estimated for the longer term. Make one person responsible for each action and agree on a firm date by which they will have completed the task. Using the action plan, generate a list of the resources in people, money, and materials required to complete the plan. Remember that you will have to persuade the managers who control the budgets and resources you need, so plan your approach. You will obviously explain the benefits that increasing sales in the account will bring to the organization, but also explain the benefits to managers and their teams. For example, will their people learn new skills if they get involved in implementing your plan? If you make your account an attractive place to work, you will improve your chances of being allocated the resources you need.

## think SMART

**Helping customers through a problem is a useful chance to build good partnerships—think of their problems as your opportunities.**

Even if the problem has nothing to do with your products or services, don't assume it is not your concern. Imagine, for example, that your customer has been unable to retain staff. To help eliminate this weakness, introduce your customer to a staff retention expert in your Human Resources team. The meeting may not produce a sale, but it is a valuable investment in the future: it will build good will and emphasize the partnership nature of your relationship with the customer.

# Summary: Writing Your Account Plan

A key account plan will help you identify the most profitable mix of products and services to sell to customers so that you can help them achieve their principal aims and objectives. Consider each customer's strategy and current situation so you can drive the plan accordingly. The basis of the account plan is the SWOT analysis—a summary of strengths, weaknesses, opportunities, and threats in relation to your customer and yourself. Thinking about the account in terms of these four key areas should give you a more realistic idea of the actions and resources you will need to achieve your objectives and help your customers to achieve theirs.

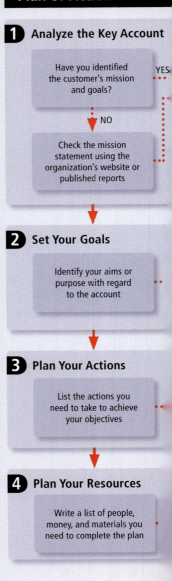

## Plan of Action

### 1 Analyze the Key Account

Have you identified the customer's mission and goals? — YES

NO ↓

Check the mission statement using the organization's website or published reports

### 2 Set Your Goals

Identify your aims or purpose with regard to the account

### 3 Plan Your Actions

List the actions you need to take to achieve your objectives

### 4 Plan Your Resources

Write a list of people, money, and materials you need to complete the plan

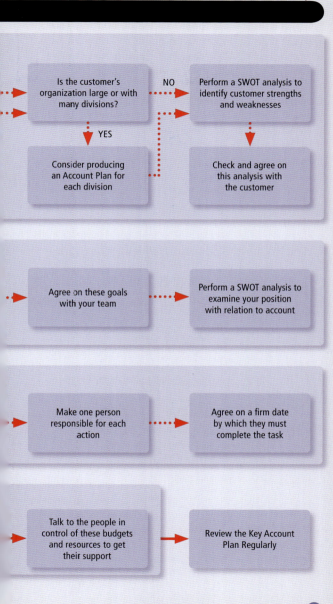

SUMMARY: WRITING YOUR ACCOUNT PLAN

# Complete the Key Account Plan

Finish the logical planning process by relating your key account plan to anyone who needs to know all, or part, of its contents. Also consider bringing in customer personnel to help build or review the plan.

## Communicate the Plan

You will have to impart your plan in some form to all the stakeholders in the account. A copy of the entire plan should go to the sales team, if you have one, and your manager, to ensure his or her commitment in helping you achieve your account objectives. An executive summary comprising two or three pages is more appropriate for others, such as senior management. Presentations must be made to key people such as the managers of the resources you require to make the plan viable: concentrate on the benefits to the organization of achieving the plan's

### Timetable for reviewing the plan

| Frequency | Activity |
|---|---|
| **Daily**<br>A few minutes | Each stakeholder reviews and updates actions for which they are responsible |
| **Weekly**<br>less than 1 hour | Each stakeholder reviews their actions and progress toward the objectives, and reports progress and potential changes to the account manager |
| **Monthly**<br>1–2 hours | Account manager reviews one or more of the objectives and action plans with the appropriate stakeholders |
| **Quarterly**<br>1–2 hours | Account manager presents progress on the account to his manager focusing on way to achieve the objectives within the time scale |
| **Half-yearly**<br>1/2–1 day | Account manager brings the team together to review the whole plan, including updating the supplier SWOT analyses |
| **Annually**<br>1–2 days | The stakeholders meet, preferably off-site, to completely redraft the plan. Ideally this will involve the customer |

**Timetable for review** Review your plan regularly to keep it up to date. Work out a timetable, such as the example above, that suits the complexity of the plan.

> ### TECHNIQUES *to* practice
>
> **Keeping planning—and other—meetings to a strict timetable is a useful skill that saves an enormous amount of time-wasting.** Remember that creating a plan is only the start. The bulk of the work is all still ahead of you. With this in mind, make sure that you do not spend more time in planning meetings than is strictly necessary. Practice this in every meeting you attend:
>
> - Agree on a finish time before, or at the start of, the meeting.
> - If the agenda is incomplete, assign individuals to complete the process individually or in small groups.
> - At the start of each meeting, briefly review what has been done since the last one.
> - Never let a meeting overrun. If necessary, schedule another appointment right after it to ensure that you finish on time.

objectives (namely increased sales) and to the staff—an interesting, rewarding job with career development opportunities through training and experience.

## Get the Customer Involved

The key element of a true partnership between a key supplier and key customer is involvement in each other's planning. It is therefore important that you make this your ultimate aim. Begin by inviting members of the customer's organization to the starting point of your Key Account Plan—the Customer's mission and purpose, and the analysis of the customer's environment or SWOT analysis. If you are working together in a culture of total trust, consider inviting them to stay while you do your own environmental analysis. Once you have completed the plan, make a presentation in which you share as much of your plan with them as you think is commercially sensible. You should also work hard on encouraging the customer to reciprocate—your goal is to be invited to join them for some of their planning meetings.

# Index

Account Development Plan 102–3
account management
  objectives 112–13
  process 102–3
action plan 60, 113
address book 30
advertising 34
after-sales service 15, 86, 87, 88
agenda, agreeing on 50
appearance, personal 16, 17

basis of decision 47, 50, 65, 69
  establishing 54
  and sales plan 61
benefits, customer 22–3, 39, 69
body language 52, 75, 76
breakeven analysis 56
building the sale 64–7
business principles 26
business process 23
buying team 58, 59

check sheets 86, 89
closing the deal 78
  handling objections 79
  summary close 78, 79
  trial close 59, 78
communicating 18–21
company profiles 27
competitors 47, 60–61, 67, 106
complaints, handling 94–5
concessions, making 77
conditions, setting 77
conferences 21
confidence 61
  developing 16, 17
  in negotiations 75
  in presentations 72
consumer markets 26
contacts 30
  broadening base 104–5
contacting suspects 36–7
conversion rate 42–3
corporate markets 27
cost/benefit analysis 59
cross-selling 92
customer 24–43
  analysis, 80/20 rule 98
  best 98–9
  development plan 101
  feedback 19
  focus 84–5
  profile 26, 38
  records 92–3
  service 85, 86, 94–5
  support 88

customer-first culture 84–5
customer need 47, 50, 69, 76
  anticipating 98–9
  establishing 53, 59
  market fit 28
  retailers 91
  and sales plan 61
  summarizing 53
customer satisfaction 14, 82–95
  measuring 86–9
  retail 90–3
  targets 105

database, customer 92–3
decision criteria *see* basis of decision
decision-maker 57–8, 70
demonstrations 64
direct mail 34, 38–9
draft project plan 55
dress 16

empathy 67, 84

feedback, customer 19, 84, 94
focus groups 88
forms 91
  and sales plan 61
  check sheets 86–7
  finance 47, 54, 56
  surveys 88
first impression 16–17
flyers 38, 39, 93
focus groups 89

goal-setting 102
growth industries 99

implementation plan 69
industrial trends 99, 100
information
  additional, seeking 60
  giving concisely 68
information sources 26
  financial press 21, 26
  Internet 26, 27, 46
inquiries 94–5
interrupting 18, 19

jargon 21

key account 94, 96–115
  plan 108–15
  process 102–3
  summary 114–15
key people 47, 57–9, 61
key stakeholders 58

leaflets 34
listening 18, 19

118 UNDERSTAND SELLING

mail, direct 34, 38–9
mailing lists 38
managers 87, 100, 101
market 26–9
market share 107
milestones 64, 65
mission statements 108, 109

negotiations 74–7
　compromising 77
　confidence 75
　identifying issues 74
　identifying needs and wants 76
　keeping calm 76
　making concessions 77
　setting conditions 77
　setting objectives 74–5

objections, handling 79
objectives
　account management 112–13
　of first call 48–9
　of negotiation 74–5
observing salespeople 15
opening the sale 50–55
　completing 60–61
　planning 48–9
　qualifying prospects 56–9
　summary 62–3
　summarizing 60
　opening sales call
　building 51
　creating 34, 37
　how to recognize 52
openings 49, 51
organizations 27
　divisions 27, 108
　promoting your own 66, 67
organizing data 30–31

planning
　draft project plan 55
　initial calls 48–9
　key account plan 108–15
　openings 49
practicality 47, 54, 61
preparation 46, 48
presentations 67, 70–3, 104, 105
price objections 79
product
　and market fit 28
　and market matrix 29
　features 22–3, 28, 66
　groups 29
　innovation 89
　knowing your 28
　returns 92
professionalism 16, 81
progress, measuring 47

promotions 34
proposal 42, 43, 67
　presenting 70–3
　structuring 69
　written 68–9
prospects 34
　contacting 35
　finding 34–5
　summary 40–1
　targeting, qualifying 56–9
　understanding 34
publicity 34
purchasing departments 23

qualifying out 56, 81
　the prospect 56–9
questionnaire 8–11
questions 18–19
　challenging 50
　closed 18, 20, 80–1, 91
　open 18, 49, 92
quotation 68

references 36, 66
relationships
　creating 14, 19
　database 92–3
　finding out about 46
　long-term, retaining 98–9
　mission and goals of 108–9
　problems of 113
resource plan 101, 102, 113
retailing 90–3
role-play 37, 49

sales assistants 91
sales calls 35
sales campaign 42, 43
sales forecast 32–3
sales pipeline 42–3, 107
sales plan 60, 61
sales process 44–81
　building sale 64–7
　clinching deal 78–9
　defining 46
　measuring performance 47
　negotiating terms 74–7
　opening call 50–63
　planning 48–9
　presenting proposal 70–3
　writing proposal 68–9
sales relationship 14–15
sales strategy 64
sales targets 32
sales team 100–1
sales techniques 15
skills, assessing 8–11
solution 47, 61
　presenting 70–3

spreadsheets 32
stakeholders 58, 100–1
  accounts 103
strategic situation 106
summary
  open the sale 62–3
  target your prospects 40–41
  write your key account plan 114–15
surveys 89
suspects 35
  contacting 36–7
  identifying 35
SWOT analysis 109, 111, 112

targets
  customer satisfaction 105
  customer service 86
  sales 31–32
telephone prospecting 35, 36–7
terms and conditions, negotiating 74–7
time, protecting 80
time management 30–31
time scale 47, 50, 54–5, 64
trade press 34

unique selling proposition (USP) 66, 67

## Picture Credits

Key: (c) = center, (r) = right, (l) = left, (t) = top, (b) = below, (bl) below left, (bc) below center, (br) = below right.

**1** Wide Group/Iconica/Getty (l), Tim McGuire/Corbis (c), Corbis (r); **2** Fabio Cardoso/Zefa/Corbis; **3** Shiva Twin/Getty (t), Ingolf Hatz/Zefa/Corbis (b), Digital Vision/Getty (c); **4** Premium Stock/Imagestate; **6** Gabe Palmer/Alamy; **8** Corbis; **3** Jon Feingersh/Zefa/Corbis; **17** Ingolf Hatz/Zefa/Corbis; **20** Don Mason/Corbis; **31** Roger Dixon/DK Images; **36** Roger Dixon/DK Images; **41** Corbis; **43** Digital Vision/Getty; **45** Premium Stock/Imagestate; **52** Roger Dixon/DK Images; **58** Fabio Cardoso/Zefa/Corbis (t), Gabe Palmer/Corbis (bl), ImageState/Alamy (bc), Walter Hodges/Getty (br); **63** Roger Dixon/DK Images; **65** Kevin Hatt/Photonica/Getty; **73** Hiep Vu/Masterfile; **78** G. Baden/Zefa/Corbis; **83** Howard Sokol/Getty; **85** Roger Dixon/DK Images; **88** Roger Dixon/DK Images; **93** Gerd George/Taxi/Getty; **97** Corbis; **101** Corbis; **110** Wide Group/Iconica/Getty.

Dorling Kindersley would like to thank the following models: Naqash Baig, Katie Dock, Caroline D'Souza.

For further information, see www.dkimages.com

## Author's Acknowledgments

Writing a book for Dorling Kindersley is a terrific exercise in teamwork. I would like to thank Adèle Hayward and Simon Tuite for their stewardship of the design and the process. Thank you also to the editor, Tom Broder, the designer, Ted Kinsey, and the rest of the editorial team for their skills, professionalism, and huge contribution. And finally, thank you all for making it such an enjoyable task.

## Author's Biography

KEN LANGDON has a background in sales and marketing in the technology industry. As an independent consultant, he has trained salespeople and sales managers in the US, Europe, and Australia and has advised managers on the coaching and appraisal of their staff. He has also provided strategic guidance for companies including computer major Hewlett Packard. Ken is the author of a number of books for DK and co-author of several Essential Managers titles, including *Putting Customers First*. He is also one of the authors of DK's *Successful Manager's Handbook*.